Eat, Skate, Win

7 Steps for Your Youth Hockey Star to
Eat Like a Champion

Kimberly Smith Lukhard, MS, RD, LDN

Copyright 2014 Kimberly Smith Lukhard, MS, RD, LDN. All rights reserved. No portion of this book may be reproduced mechanically, electronically, or by any other means, including photocopying, without written permission of the publisher. It is illegal to copy this book, post it to a website, or distribute it by any other means without permission from the publisher.

Kimberly Smith Lukhard, MS, RD, LDN
kim@HockeyMomRD.com
www.HockeyMomRD.com

ISBN: 978-1-4975-9281-0

Limits of Liability and Disclaimer of Warranty

The author and publisher shall not be liable for your misuse of this material. This book is strictly for informational and educational purposes.

Warning – Disclaimer

The purpose of this book is to educate and entertain. The author and/or publisher do not guarantee that anyone following these techniques, suggestions, tips, ideas, or strategies will become successful. The author and/or publisher shall have neither liability nor responsibility to anyone with respect to any loss or damage caused, or alleged to be caused, directly or indirectly by the information contained in this book.

Unleash the Champion in Your Youth Hockey Star!

Discover the secrets to help your child be a champion on the ice and in the classroom. During your phone "chalk talk" sessions you will find out how to apply action steps to unleash the future NHL player in your youth hockey star.

Do you want your child to…

- Avoid a midmorning energy crash in school?

- Have a body well fueled to hit the ice?

- Have lasting energy on the ice?

- Build stronger skating muscle?

- Learn how food can be as important as sharp skates and his hockey stick?

If you answered YES, get started at HockeyMomRD.com and grab your three power recipes. There you will also find other tips and resources to make your hockey player a star.

Testimonials

"Recommended Her to My Hockey Family!"

I received a specialized plan from Kim for my first-year Bantam just before the season began. She included allergies/preferences as well as late adjustments for dislike of all things peanut. It has truly helped us all make positive changes toward better meal plans that incorporate the specialized needs of a hockey player. I couldn't be more pleased with the plan and the personalized service I received, and I have recommended her to all my hockey family! Thanks to Hockey Mom RD!

~ Shelleigh Killian

"As a Physician, I Am Impressed!"

My daughter lives by the plan Kim worked out for her this fall and I can't say thank you enough! Maggie is away from home at the Ontario Hockey Academy and has a rigorous strength training routine and on-ice practice every single day. Kim gave her great practical guidelines on how to choose foods to meet her nutritional needs and food preferences specific to her situation. As a mother I am so glad she has Kim's guidance away from me. As a physician I am impressed by Kim's total approach and in-depth plans. I commend Hockey Mom RD and recommend her evaluation and advice for youth athletes in any sport.

~ Elizabeth Blair, MD, PhD

"Kim Created Thoughtful and Detailed Plans"

Our boys have been playing (and loving!) hockey since long before they could spell their own names. Once we became a hockey family, there was no looking back! One piece of the puzzle that has always been difficult for us as parents is nutrition. Are our boys eating enough of the right foods? How long before a game should they have a snack and what should that snack be? Kim created thoughtful and detailed plans for both of my boys that answered every question we ever had and so many more. We feel so much more confident as hockey parents that our boys are fueled up and hydrated so that they can play to their full potential and have as much fun as possible on and off the ice! Did I mention that Kim is registered dietician, a college professor working with student athletes, as well as a hockey mom and player? Well, really, what more could you ask for?

~ Ellie Petrov, hockey mom and blogger (www.Creative-Geekery.com)

For Dad

You taught me nothing is impossible when I decide to do it.

About the Author

Kim is a mother of two energetic hockey players, dietitian, IYCA-certified youth nutrition specialist, and university professor. She watched her first ice hockey game when her younger brother started playing after her family relocated to Connecticut from North Carolina. Throughout her teenage years Kim lived at the rink in the wintertime. She and her brother would be dropped off in the morning and skate all day. She loved being a "rink rat."

Despite spending college years in Boston, Massachusetts, she never saw a Bruins game.

Kim was reintroduced to the game when one of her students invited her and her boys to an ice hockey game at ECU in 2008. The moment she heard the sound of the skates on the ice she was hooked, and so were her sons. Kim earned her BA in psychology from Simmons College in Boston, Massachusetts, and her MS in nutrition science from East Carolina University in Greenville, North Carolina. She completed her dietetic internship at the Brody School of Medicine in Greenville, North Carolina.

Kim has been a member of the nutrition faculty at East Carolina University since 2001.

Her mission is to bring out the champion in your skater by teaching you how to fuel your skater before, during, and after practices and games. The seven steps discussed in this book will bring out the champion in your child on the ice and in the classroom.

Contents

Preface 1

Introduction Back to the Rink: Let the Season Begin! 3

Part I Introducing the Starting Lineup 5

   Step 1 9

      In Net: Water: Liquid Gold 9

   The Power Nutrients: On the Offense 15

      Right Wing: Carbohydrates 15

      Center: Protein 20

      Left Wing: Fat 27

   Meet the Defensive Line: Vitamins and Minerals 35

      Vitamins 35

      Minerals 47

Part II Let the Game Begin 57

   Step 2: Water: How to Calculate Your Skater's Needs 59

   Step 3: Carbohydrates: How to Choose the Best Energy Foods ... 63

   Step 4: Protein: Eat for Skating Power 67

   Step 5: Road Trip 71

   Step 6: Fueling for Game Day 77

   Step 7: Time to Organize 81

Recipes 87

Conclusion **101**

Resources **103**

Testimonials **105**

Preface

It is hard to believe that I have been a hockey mom for over five years. There have been six-hour trips in the car, 4:30 a.m. wakeup calls for 6 a.m. games, cold rinks, and always smiling faces on the kids. As a hockey mom, I have done it all: I have filled water bottles, provided snacks, fetched equipment, texted the manager of the team while manning the penalty box to inform her that our team will get a 10-minute penalty unless three of our players get the helmet straps that are missing. I have tied countless pairs of skates for the Mites, Squirts, and Pee Wees, tightened and adjusted helmets, run the clock, and kept score. Can you relate?

Thoughout the years I have answered many nutrition questions and provided my team with nutrition guidance. As a dietitian I view the human body as a marvelous machine. I have taught my boys about food and their body. They have learned that their performance on the ice and in the class is affected by what they have or have not eaten.

I wrote this book for you, hockey moms and dads. Now you can have a "hockey nutritionist" with you at all times.

I have written this book in two parts. In Part I you will learn about the six nutrients that are crucial for your youth hockey player's success on and off the ice. I will introduce you to the starting lineup that works hard inside your skater's body. I know you are familiar with the six members of the hockey team: winger, center, and winger on the offensive line, two defensive players, and goalie. The six nutrients you will learn about are carbohydrates, protein, and fats, on the offensive line. Why? All of these nutrients provide calories so your skater's body can skate and think. The vitamins and minerals are the body's defense, helping to fight off illness and infection. These defensemen aid in keeping your player strong for the game. And last but not least, water. Water is an indispensable, multitasking nutrient, with many jobs. At the end of Part I you will have a greater understanding of nutrition and how it can help support your hockey player's goals on and off the ice.

In Part II you will learn how to apply the information to help pick the best combination of foods before games, in between games, and after games. You will learn how to revamp your pantry, refrigerator, and freezer, and how to make hockey strong choices when you are traveling. I have even included a generic meal plan for your reference.

By the time you finish this book you will have learned much of what I teach my nutrition students each semester. You will understand how fueling your youth hockey player with great food can be more important to his success on the ice than a $180 stick. You will understand that while kids may love candy, Skittles, and Pixy Stix, these are not as good as a banana or grapes before a game. When your skater insists on an energy drink because "all the other kids get to drink one," you will know why it is in your skater's best health interest to make sure he doesn't follow the crowd. My goal is to provide you with the information that enables you to make the best choices for your child starting today. From this day forward your child will be prepared for tryouts, tournaments, and all the quizzes, tests, and exams he will face in the future.

No time to waste—let's begin.

Introduction

Back to the Rink: Let the Season Begin!

It begins when you pull into the rink parking lot. You can't help but think to yourself, *What will this season bring?*

If you listen for a moment you can almost hear your skater's thoughts: *Will I be the tallest and fastest this year?* Then the questions begin, and you haven't even parked the car: "Mom, do you think I will be faster than #23 this year? Do you think we will win the championship this year?" Your skater's thoughts continue at lightning speed, as you pull into the parking space. "I hope we have a great team this year; I really want to finish in first. I am so excited I can feel it running through my veins. I have great hopes for the new season; I know we can do it this year!"

The car is finally parked and you open the trunk to your car. Your kid pulls out his bag and sticks. Before you shut the trunk, he is running to the rink door, his giant, 30-pound hockey bag on his shoulder. You open the door for your kid and walk from 75 degrees to 45 degrees, you see the ice, you hear the blades cutting the ice as the players skate by, and you catch a whiff of a hockey bag you know wasn't unpacked during the off-season—you are home! Another season has begun. You are back in the icy environment where you know you will live for the next five months or more. You catch up with hockey friends you haven't seen all summer as your skaters get dressed for their first practice of the new season. It is a new beginning, everyone is happy, and you and your skater love it.

As you watch the first practice you know your player's body is pumped with adrenaline and you think to yourself, *Could this be the season the team makes it to the championship playoffs?* You reflect on last season, how the team finished in the standings, and you think to yourself, *Maybe this season if the team practices harder, if they have more drills, more scrimmages, more offensive, defensive, and goalie clinics, maybe this year we will make it.*

You drift off as the practice continues and find yourself in your own thoughts. *I am so happy hockey season is back, but how is our family going to manage the schedule?* Then the to-do list starts to run through your brain—grocery list, scheduled homework before practice or in the car on the way to practice, what weekends you will be traveling—and you remember that slow cooker dinners will save the day. You try to stay in the moment, just focusing on your skater, but as a parent you have to make sure your player maintains good grades and performs to the best of his ability at each practice and game.

All of these great thoughts you and your skater are having pave the way to the championship playoffs, yet one ingredient is missing from your championship recipe.

That missing ingredient is nutrition. I know that sounds dry and boring, but stay with me here! Team nutritionists with the American Hockey League meet with new players to help them learn what foods to eat to support their body's hockey needs. Nutrition is key to fueling your hockey player one practice at a time, one game at a time, one plate at a time, to give him the edge to develop and become a champion.

Are you ready to learn how to add this key ingredient to your skater's championship recipe?

Part I
Introducing the Starting Lineup

You know the feeling, the National Anthem has just been sung and the fans are cheering as they wait with anticipation to hear the announcement of the starting lineup. There isn't a hockey player alive who doesn't dream of hearing his name and number called for the starting lineup. It takes months for some, and years for others to be a part of the first line. There are countless practices and games before the big day.

There is a starting lineup of another kind that is in reach of all hockey players, no matter their age or level of play. This lineup consists of six nutrients: carbohydrates, protein, fats, vitamins, minerals, and water. These are the players that fuel your hockey player. These six nutrients give your skater the power, speed, endurance, focus, and stamina to make it to the starting lineup.

If you help your skater learn what I have written in this book, championship food choices will become second nature to him as he grows and plays hockey.

In Part I you will learn water is essential. Carbohydrates, protein, and fats provide your skater with calories, and vitamins and minerals work offensively in the body to aid in turning food into energy, and defensively to support his immune system.

By the end of Part I you will see that the nutrient team of six on the inside is the starting lineup for your hockey player's success on the ice.

Before you picked up this book maybe you thought nutrition was only about weight loss, counting points, measuring portion sizes, and stepping on the scale. You were already very familiar with that type of nutrition. The nutrition section of the bookstore may be the place you spend the most time. In this book you will learn the science of nutrition and how it can make your skater a starter.

Let's take a closer look. What is nutrition? Pick up any textbook and you will learn that nutrition is the science of how your body uses the foods and fluids you consume to keep it going. Do you want your second-year Bantam to be the one the coach is afraid to put on the ice with two minutes left in the third period when your team is down by one goal? This might have been okay with you when your skater was a Mite or a Squirt, but now you know your child wants to play varsity ice hockey in college, at least. As you become more knowledgeable about the science of nutrition you can educate your skater about how to make more hockey-supportive choices. I know your skater wants to be fast, powerful, and strong, and a smart skater on the ice. Nutrition can impact all of those qualities positively or negatively.

What do all of these teams have in common: Anaheim Ducks, Boston Bruins, Calgary Flames, Carolina Hurricanes, Chicago Blackhawks, Colorado Avalanche, Dallas Stars, Detroit Red Wings, Edmonton Oilers, Los Angeles Kings, Montreal Canadians, New Jersey Devils, New York Islanders, New York Rangers, Ottawa Senators, Philadelphia Flyers, Pittsburgh Penguins, Tampa Bay Lightning, and Toronto Maple Leafs? A Stanley Cup—at least one.

These teams also have a team dietitian who educates them on championship food choices. How many times have you heard your hockey player say he wants to play in the NHL? Or make the Olympic team? Don't you want the same nutrition education for your hockey player? Championship food choices must become a habit for your child. The sooner your skater learns how his food choices impact his hockey game, the better. When these food choices become second nature to your skater, he will be prepared for tryouts, tournaments, and all the quizzes, tests, and exams he will face in his future.

Flashback to tryouts, a nerve-racking time for the parents. All parents brings their skater ready to give it 200 percent. They have made sure their skater has practiced and skated during the off-season. However, many times a child isn't fueled like a champion before tryouts. I know that time and nerves get in the way of choosing the best foods, but stop and think for a minute, and imagine the worst-case scenario. You have had the work week from hell. Projects continue to come in with deadlines, your youngest has been sick, and you have to put in extra hours to catch up. You look at your calendar and realize tryouts are tomorrow! You think to yourself,

How did I let this happen? You take a breath, and make sure the hockey bag is packed. You know the skates are sharp; you just had them sharpened before your player's private lesson the other day. Now it's time to go. You grab a soda and a part of a leftover sub sandwich from the day before, and hit the road for the rink. You think, *Gosh, I know I could have fed him something better, but we ran out of time.* As you drive you have hopes your child will make the AAA team. Tryouts begin and your hockey player is skating well, until suddenly his right hamstring gets a major cramp and sends him falling to the ice in the middle of a timed speed drill! You watch and think, *Oh no!! This is not how I imagined it.*

Or consider this scenario: You have to pick your skater up from school and drive straight to tryouts. He is starving so you stop for food an hour before tryouts begin. Your skater eats a large meal to calm the hunger pains. But in the middle of a practice scrimmage during tryouts, he vomits through his cage, onto the ice, and tryouts are stopped to quickly clean up the mess! I know you might be thinking, *Gee, I was only trying to help him and make sure he was well fed before practice.*

Now imagine the best-case scenario: Tryouts are two weeks away. You know your hockey player has dreams of making the AAA team this year. You have repeated many times, "You do the work on the ice, and I will drive you to practices and games." In preparation for tryouts you go to the grocery store and buy fruits, yogurt, vegetables, pasta, milk, nuts, and some lean meats. You make sure you have tons of water available to quickly grab as you run out the door or when the kids come in from playing outside. This time you leave the soda and chips on the shelf in the store. You want to stock your house with power foods! Those two weeks go by fast. Tryouts are Saturday, but this year you are calmer. Why? You know you and your skater have done the prep work going into tryouts. And guess what? Your player makes the AAA team!

Which of these three scenarios do you want to see play out in the upcoming ice hockey season?? I know you would vote 100 percent for the best-case scenario for your youth ice hockey player.

So how can you ensure you and your skater leave the rink achieving the best-case scenario?

Dive into this book and soak up all the information. I am going to show you how to make sure your skater is fueled like a champion with protein, carbohydrates, fats, vitamins, minerals, and water, each day. You may even learn some information you want to apply to your own workout and life. By the time you finish reading this book you *will* be able to fuel your child like a champion *all* of the time.

Step 1

In Net: Water: Liquid Gold

Water and the goalie have one thing in common: Each has many jobs to perform. If you are new to ice hockey you may see the goalie as the one who stops the puck from going into the net. But if you are a seasoned hockey mom or dad, you know the goalie has many jobs; being the last line of defense is just one of them. The goalie can stop a play, get a penalty, start a play, and even score a goal. The goalie is similar to water, in that both have many jobs to perform.

Liquid gold—water. It drips off your player's face as he steps off the ice. You can't miss your player's shower-soaked head of hair when the helmet comes off; you know your skater is thirsty. It is hard to believe your youth hockey player can lose a pound or more of water weight during a practice, but he can.

Let's take a closer look at water. A glass of water can be the key that unlocks your child's championship abilities. What? That sounds so simple! Well, it is, if you understand the importance of water and what water will do for the body besides merely quenching thirst.

Before I go any further, I want you to know that if you are thirsty you are already dehydrated. Yes, by the time your brain tells you, "Drink. I need water," you have already lost 1 percent of your body weight. For a skater weighing 100 pounds, that is only 1 pound. And 1 pound of weight loss on the scale is equal to 2 cups of water. A small water loss can have big consequences on the ice and in the classroom.

To begin, water is the most indispensable nutrient. Your body cannot survive without water. Water is simply an inorganic liquid comprised of two hydrogen and one water molecules. An adult's body is 60 percent water, a child's body is 70 percent water, and an infant's body is 75 percent water. Did you know your brain and heart are 73 percent water, your lungs are 83 percent water, your skin is 64 percent water, your muscles and kidneys are 79 percent water, and your bones are 31 percent water? You can see that water is everywhere in your body and in your skater's body, too.

The more muscle you have on your body, the more water you need. Now can you see why water is the most indispensable nutrient? Water or the lack of water impacts many systems.

Water is a multitasking nutrient with many jobs to perform:

- Water carries nutrients throughout your body.

- Water is a solvent. It helps to dissolve the vitamins, minerals, amino acids, and glucose from the food you eat, so those nutrients can be carried throughout your body.

- Water helps rid your body of waste by cleansing your tissues and blood.

- Water participates in chemical reactions in your body. The water molecule is always being built or broken apart.

- Water helps lubricate your joints.

- Water is a shock absorber inside your eyes, spinal cord, and joints, and your youth ice hockey player started in a bag of water (the amniotic sac).

- Water helps regulate your body's temperature.

Imagine what would happen if you neglected to drink water. I forgot to mention that keeping your body well hydrated can even make those little "lines of wisdom" on your face look better. The water bottle is an essential piece of equipment, just like a pair of sharp skates. The sharp skates are needed so your player can outskate the other team's players on the way to the net, but without water, those strong skating muscles will not perform at championship level.

Remember: Muscles are 79 percent water. A thirsty muscle will not perform the way you want it to. If you've ever gone for a morning run or jog, you know what I mean.

Imagine the feeling of lead in your muscles before you get ready to go for your morning run. You want to run your best time, but this time you were too busy to pay attention to what you "didn't" drink. Before you are even halfway finished with your morning run, your legs get heavy, they are hard to move, and you feel wiped out! Is this how you want your skater to feel on the ice? *No!* Imagine this: You are watching the game, your skater comes out of the box for his shift on the ice, you see the puck glide right in front of your child, and a player from the other team outskates your child, grabs the puck, and scores! How did that happen? Start with water. Your child's muscles may have been thirsty. Thirsty muscles do not perform at championship level, during practice or a game. And even worse, thirsty muscles will cramp. I know you don't want your child's hamstring muscle seizing up when he is on a breakaway down the ice with the puck in a scoring situation.

And one last problem: Balance can be impacted by lack of fluid. I can't name a hockey player who wants his balance affected when skating on a 1/8-inch blade. Did you know that youth hockey players can lose up to 2 quarts of water a day? That is 64 ounces (1.9 liters). They need to replenish their body's water supply all day long.

Thirsty muscles are just the beginning. A dehydrated skater will not be able to focus. If you are thirsty you have lost between 1 and 3 percent of your body weight, and you are considered mildly dehydrated. For example, let's assume you weigh 135 pounds. If you were mildly dehydrated that would mean you had lost between 1.3 and 3.9 pounds; let's say 4 pounds. In cups, that is between 3 and 8 cups of water.

Your body needs water before you are thirsty. In addition to thirst, your memory might be foggy, your muscles will not perform during your exercise routine, and you may feel tired. Studies have shown that athletic performance can be compromised at 1-percent loss of body weight. Now imagine your child beginning a practice or a game in the same condition. I know you would never wish that on your player.

Remember the play your child went over and over in his head, and practiced multiple times on the ice? It might as well have been written with invisible ink, because a dehydrated brain will not think, or remember, as well as a hydrated brain. The brain is 73 percent water.

Focus and memory will be impacted even more when your skater gets a headache from lack of water. *No,* it isn't the helmet. If your child has a headache, the helmet may not be too tight; it may be that your child needs more water.

Do an experiment. When your child comes home from school ask him how much he drank in school. If he is like most children, he probably only drank the juice box you packed with his snack, and the milk, water, or juice he had with lunch. In a six- to seven-hour school day, if that is all your child drinks, he has consumed at best 16 ounces of fluid. (Juice boxes are usually 6 ounces, and milk cartons are only 8 ounces.)

Now let's look at what your child actually needs.

Daily Water Needs for Boys and Girls		
	Age Range	Minimum Amount Needed
Boys	4–8 years	7, 8-ounce glasses (1.7 L)
	9–13 years	10, 8-ounce glasses (2.4 L)
Girls	4–8 years	7, 8-ounce glasses (1.7 L)
	9–13 years	9, 8-ounce glasses (2.2 L)

You may be thinking, *My child doesn't like to drink water.* Fear not. Fluids like milk and juice count in your child's water intake for the day. And even better, some fruits and vegetables are rich in water. Does your child like watermelon or cantaloupe? Wonderful! These fruits are packed with water—more than 90 percent. If your child isn't a fan of watermelon or cantaloupe, how about apricots, blueberries, oranges, peaches, pineapples, plums, and raspberries, which contain more than 85 percent water? And I can't leave the water-rich vegetables off my list. Celery, cucumbers, iceberg lettuce, tomatoes, zucchini, broccoli, green cabbage, cauliflower, eggplant, and spinach are rich in water, too.

Water is crucial to your child's performance on the ice. It doesn't matter if you buy the newest, lightest skate, and the best stick, and equipment; if his body is just 1 percent dehydrated, his athletic ability will be impacted. Are you starting to remember that small percentage? It is easy to underestimate the importance of water, but don't.

One last thought about fluids: Energy drinks are not a good choice for your skater. While these drinks contain water and some added vitamins, these drinks also contain caffeine, much more caffeine than a 12-ounce soda. I am sure you have heard these drinks can be dangerous, especially when coupled with exercise. Children are naturally loaded with energy.

Now you are armed with the information you and your skater need to ensure his growing body is well hydrated before, during, and after practices and games. Encourage your skater to stay well hydrated and he will have greater successes on the ice and in the classroom.

The Power Nutrients: On the Offense

The offensive line on a hockey team skates very fast. Watch any hockey game and you will see how the players go from standing still, waiting in position at the faceoff, to skating at lightning speed after the puck drops. Your player needs to eat carbohydrates to be fueled for speed, regardless of the position he plays.

Right Wing: Carbohydrates

Believe it or not, you probably take better care of your car than your body. You may be thinking to yourself, *No, I don't,* but stay with me a moment. Would you try to drive your car if the fuel needle was on empty? I don't know about you, but when my car's fuel gauge registers a quarter of a tank I fill up. In the winter I try not to let the needle fall below half a tank. Your body is like a car; it needs fuel to run. Without enough fuel your body will come to a rapid stop, too. But unlike a car, your body doesn't have a fuel gauge, so you can easily run your "tank" too low to function at your best.

Stop and think for a moment. I bet you know at least one friend who has tried to cut out carbohydrates in an attempt to lose weight. But what happens? She ends up feeling tired and moody, and has no energy for her workouts. Why? Carbohydrates are the body's "go-to" source for energy. Carbohydrates are sugars, starches, fibers, and glycogen (the human and animal body's storage form of glucose).

Carbohydrates provide 4 calories per gram. Carbohydrates are huge molecules made of many single glucose molecules strung together. Imagine a necklace of M & M's. Each one of those M & M's is a glucose molecule, a simple sugar. The energized feeling you experience when you eat M & M's is due to the rapid absorption of glucose into your bloodstream. Your body can use it immediately.

Your brain is designed to run only on glucose, which is supplied from the carbohydrates you eat. To keep you pushing through your practice, game, or workout, your muscles depend on carbohydrates, too. Carbohydrates help your muscles to use stored glycogen supplies more slowly. Without enough carbohydrates your muscles quickly deplete their glycogen supply and you lose your steam. Cutting out carbohydrates is not the answer.

Carbohydrates are classified as simple (monosaccharide and disaccharide) or complex (starch, glycogen, and fiber), and are comprised of single or multiple sugars. To understand carbohydrates better it is important to know that there are six sugar molecules in the carbohydrates you eat. The single-sugar molecules are classified as monosaccharides: glucose, fructose, and galactose. The two-sugar molecules are classified as lactose, maltose, and sucrose. Simple carbohydrates are found in milk, fruit, refined sugar products, honey, and fruit juices. Note that milk and fruit are in the simple carbohydrate category. Milk contains lactose (a disaccharide) and fruit contains fructose (a monosaccharide). All disaccharides contain glucose and another monosaccharide. Here I want to make the point that all simple carbohydrates are not equal. Milk and fruit are excellent choices for you and your hockey player before and after exercise.

Keep in mind not all monosaccharides are great before a game. Yes, all monosaccharides provide quick energy, but your hockey player needs quick, sustaining energy. I have seen young players go to the snack bar just before practice, take a small, 4-ounce cup of water, and add four or five packets of sugar. Sugar water—sure, it is quick energy, for a while, but the energy burst is followed by an equally quick and dramatic energy crash. Practices are important. This is where the players learn the drills and plays, and work on gaining stamina so they can perform at 100 percent during games. Imagine your star skater fueling with sugar water before a game, only to lose his speed on a breakaway to score the first goal of the game. Now imagine if that was the championship game. Would you want your skater fueling on fruit or Pixy Stix?

Complex carbohydrates are found in starches, fiber, and glycogen. Starch is found in potatoes, rice, corn, peas, legumes (such as black beans and garbanzo beans), bread, and quinoa. Glycogen is your body's storage form of glucose. You store glycogen in your muscles for the exercise you do, and your liver stores glycogen to aid in keeping your blood sugar stable in between meals.

Now let me apply all that nutrition science for you. It is no secret that carbohydrates are great to eat before you exercise. However, choosing the correct type is very important.

Did you know your muscles can use the glucose from the broken-down carbohydrates three times quicker than energy from fat? Now that you know this, just imagine your next race; instead of that sausage biscuit an hour before the race begins, choose oatmeal with milk, brown sugar, and a banana. You will be amazed at the sustained energy you will have.

Not to mention, if you are not fueling your body with carbohydrates, your muscle cells will not have the glycogen stores needed to fuel your next run. You need your muscles to be packed with glycogen so you can get the most out of your run. If you exercise hard for two hours, you need to replenish your glycogen stores. It takes your body about two hours to deplete your glycogen stores.

Studies have compared runners on three different diets: high fat (94 percent fat, 6 percent protein), normal (55 percent carbohydrate), and high carbohydrate (83 percent carbohydrate). The runners consuming the high-fat diet were only able to run for 57 minutes; the normal diet, 114 minutes; and the high-carbohydrate diet, 167 minutes! Which runner would you like to be?

Now imagine a scenario for your youth hockey player. You pick your child up from school and head to practice. The last time he ate was at noon. It is now 3:30 p.m., and practice begins at 5 p.m. You have some peanut butter crackers in the car but nothing more. "Oh, you will be fine. Just eat these and get some water at the rink," you say to your child. Practice begins and he is doing well, yet 30 minutes into the one-and-a-half-hour practice he starts to fade, he loses his speed, and he just can't seem to catch his second wind. What happened? His body needed more fuel in the form of carbohydrates.

Imagine this worst-case scenario: In the middle of a game you look over and see all the hockey players on the bench, actively watching the game, play by play, so they know what to do when it is time for their line to go on. Then suddenly, without warning, one of the young players falls sideways onto the bench. Scary! You know it isn't your child, but it is one of your son's teammates. You find out that the child had severe low blood sugar and passed out. He had been sick a few days before the game and wasn't able to eat like he normally did prior to his games.

Fiber is a member of the carbohydrate family that is often overlooked. *Wait a minute,* you might be thinking. *I thought fiber was only important to us older folks.* True, fiber is very important to all the parents reading, and fiber is very important to our children, too. There are two types of fiber: soluble and insoluble. I am sure you have seen the Cheerios commercial where the daughter places Cheerios in her dad's coat pocket and briefcase before his trip. Why? Not because she is afraid her daddy will get hungry, but because she wants him to have a healthy heart. Cheerios contain soluble fiber, which is beneficial for your heart health and helps to reduce your blood cholesterol.

Insoluble fiber is a part of the fruit, vegetable, or whole grain that the human body can't digest; we do not have the enzymes. Insoluble fiber makes you feel full longer, helps to control blood sugar levels, and helps to fight constipation. This type of fiber is used by the colon to make more than 400 different types of beneficial bacteria that live in our gut. Why is this important? I know a few of you reading have seen hockey players bleed on the ice (scary, especially if the player injured is your child). Did you know that vitamin K, the clotting vitamin, is made by bacteria in our gut? Now you can see that fiber is not only about keeping your heart healthy, and keeping you comfortable because you will not be constipated, but fiber helps to ensure that supply of vitamin K is there when needed to slow down and stop the bleeding (unless, of course, stitches are needed).

A word of caution with fiber: Too much can be harmful on the ice. Why? When your player is fueling for a game it is natural to reach for cereal, especially early in the morning. It's quick, it's filling, and it powers your skater for the game. If you don't choose the cereal carefully you may unintentionally overload your hockey player with too much fiber. Normally this wouldn't be a big problem, but before a game or practice it is. Too much fiber can cause abdominal cramps and discomfort; both take away from the ability to focus on skating and winning.

Imagine this scenario: The team makes it all the way to the playoff game for the championship title. The game is scheduled for 6 a.m., which means you have to be at the rink by 5 a.m. You rush to breakfast at the hotel, and they have set up a grab-and-go-style breakfast. Your player grabs a box of fiber-rich cereal (3 g or greater), and you think nothing of it. You arrive at the rink on time. Players are dressed, the puck drops, and 10 minutes into the first 15-minute period your player asks to leave the ice. He can't stand up straight. He didn't take a hit; his cramps are so bad he can't play. Yes, this can happen.

It is important to remember that carbohydrates are your body's fuel. You wouldn't want to put water-laced gasoline in your car's engine. Pick the long-lasting carbohydrates. Foods like potatoes, fruits, oatmeal, pasta, and wild rice are good choices. These foods give you sustained energy, unlike the quick-acting carbohydrates in sugary candy, cookies, and cakes. Stock your kitchen with vegetables and whole-wheat breads, and pastas for you and your child. This step will insure you are eating the fiber you need each day. As a guideline, adults need 25–35 grams of fiber a day, and your skater needs his age + 5 grams. So my 11-year-old Pee Wee needs 16 grams of fiber each day.

There is one more point I need to make about carbohydrates, so stay with me. I am sure you have heard some people say, "Oh, don't eat carrots. They contain too much sugar." Carrots are a low-calorie, low-carbohydrate vegetable choice that provides only 25 calories per medium carrot and 203 percent of the daily vitamin A needed. Don't avoid them; plus your eyes will thank you. You may be asking yourself, *If carrots are so good for you, then why do some people make the statement that carrots are high in sugar?* Let me explain. There is an index that compares 50 grams of a specific food to 50 grams of table sugar to see how the specific food raises your blood sugar when compared to the table sugar. That index is the Glycemic Index. There is another index, which I prefer, entitled the Glycemic Load Index. This index measures how quickly a true serving of food will cause your blood sugar to rise. I will try to help you understand.

Flash to breakfast-time at any away game: It is 6 a.m. and all the sleepy hockey players are crowding around the waffle maker while the parents are sitting with their cups of coffee and talking or reading the paper. Waffles are typically the breakfast of choice for my hockey players. Using the Glycemic Index, 50 grams of waffles would cause blood sugar to spike very fast. Remember that a rapid rise or spike in blood sugar is followed by an equally rapid crash—not what you want for your player. However, using the Glycemic Load Index, one waffle (equivalent to a 4-inch frozen waffle) will raise blood sugar gradually and sustain your player's energy. If he adds syrup to that waffle, the rate at which blood sugar spikes will increase; if he adds butter or any other fat, the waffle will create a slower blood sugar spike. (In Step 6, I cover specifics about food and fueling on a game day.)

I hope by now you are beginning to see the importance of carbohydrates. On game days more than half of the food your skater eats should come from carbohydrate-rich food choices.

Next you will learn about protein, an important team player for your skater's growing body.

Center: Protein

When the puck drops every team depends on their center to win the faceoff and start the play. Protein can be thought of as the center of your food choices. Protein keeps your hunger pains away, helping you to keep running, and helping your hockey player to stay focused and strong during his practice or game.

If you are the parent of a second-year Pee Wee or Bantam, you may be starting to hear some of the players talk about putting on weight, especially the boys. Or maybe this scene is being played out in your home: It is dinnertime and you have cooked some yummy stir-fry chicken with vegetables and rice. You serve your rapidly growing hockey player what you think is a good serving, and all but the plate is devoured in less than five minutes and he is asking for more. But that isn't the end. No, after rapidly consuming a second helping of dinner, an hour goes by and you hear, "Mom, I am hungry." I know you are thinking, *Oh my goodness. He just ate; how can he be hungry again?* When children hit this age they are bottomless pits. (My mom used to say, "Where is your hollow leg? You must have one for all the food you are eating.")

In this section you will learn all about protein and its many jobs. In addition you will learn about animal and vegetarian sources of protein you can include in your skater's food plan. In Part II of this book I teach you how to determine the amount of protein your child needs each day during the season and off-season.

What is protein? From a nutritionist's perspective, protein is one of three macronutrients (carbohydrates and fats are the other two). It provides you with calories—4 calories/gram, to be exact. To help you see this, a piece of lunch meat that you use to make a sandwich for your child is 1 ounce, which equals 28.5 grams. Now do the math: 28.5 g x 4 calories/gram = 114 calories in that 1 ounce of luncheon meat, not to mention 7 g of protein. Your growing hockey player needs these calories and protein.

Let me translate.

Protein molecules are large and made out of amino acids; these are the building blocks of proteins. Just as you create your shopping list one item at a time for the meals you will cook, your body builds proteins one amino acid at a time based on the job the protein needs to accomplish. You wouldn't substitute ingredients in a recipe, and your body is the same way with the proteins it builds. To understand how proteins are made I need to take you back to sixth-grade science. I am sure you remember studying the human cell, and you recall the nucleus is the place where your DNA is housed. When you were conceived, you received half of your DNA from your mother and half from your father. Why is this important? The blueprint for all the jobs proteins do in your body begins in the DNA. I know you usually associate protein consumption with muscle growth, but protein has many jobs.

Protein's many jobs include:

- Making collagen in our skin, teeth, ligaments, and tendons, and helping to keep your hair, fingernails, and bones strong.

- Helping with chemical reactions during digestion.

- Helping with movement of your body, because protein is found in muscle, tendons, and ligaments.

- Helping to transport nutrients in and out of your cells and throughout your body via the bloodstream. Calcium, glucose, sodium, and vitamin A are some of the nutrients that get help from these protein transporters.

- Helping tissues and organs communicate to keep your body healthy. Did you know many of the hormones in your body are proteins? Insulin and glucagon, the two hormones that aid in blood sugar homeostasis or balance, are proteins.

- Helping to make antibodies to fight off infection.
- Helping to make sure your body doesn't have too much fluid in the tissues (edema).
- And helping your blood maintain a healthy pH level so your body isn't too acidic or too alkaline.

Yes, I just gave you a mini physiology lesson. Now you can see that proteins are not only for building muscles. When your child gets a cut, his blood will begin to clot because there are clotting proteins that help make sure the bleeding stops. This sets up the first barrier of protection from infection. Next his body's protein messengers fly into action, making collagen for the scar tissue by using the recipe sent from his DNA in the nucleus of his cell.

I know you have had days where you couldn't stop to eat because you were so busy. During those busy times your body is producing glucagon, a hormone that helps to maintain your blood sugar level in between meals. Once you get a chance to finally eat, your body is using some proteins to make enzymes that will aid in the digestion of that long-awaited meal.

There are 20 players on the protein team; all are amino acids. Just as your child's team has different plays to achieve different results, these proteins come together in various combinations to accomplish their wide variety of jobs. Nine of these amino acids are classified as essential. This means you must obtain these amino acids from the foods you eat; your body cannot make them. These amino acids are: histidine, isoleucine, leucine, lysine, methionine, phenylalanine, threonine, tryptophan, and valine.

The remaining 11 amino acids are classified as non-essential; you do not have to get these amino acids from your diet; your body can make these from the essential amino acids. Non-essential amino acids are: alanine, arginine, asparagine, aspartic acid, cysteine, glutamic acid, glutamine, glycine, proline, serine, and tyrosine.

Now the next time you eat your favorite meal, you can imagine all the jobs the protein will be working on. You have something in common with these proteins: Proteins multitask for your body, and you multitask for your family each day. You, like the proteins, complete many jobs without much notice from others.

What if My Child Is a Vegetarian?

If you have a child that doesn't like meat, or has chosen to try vegetarianism, don't panic. Your child will be able to consume all the protein he needs without meat.

Imagine this scenario:

One day your hockey player comes to you and announces, "Mom, Dad, I am going to be a vegetarian." Don't look at your child like he has three heads, even if you know his favorite food is bacon. After all, the gorilla, the king of the jungle, is a vegan! This is a time to support his decision. Your child is beginning to make more and more of his own decisions, and it is your job to guide, support, and teach him. A vegetarian is a person who chooses not to eat any flesh of the animal. This includes fish. A vegetarian who consumes milk and eggs from animals is referred to as a lacto-ovo vegetarian. A vegan does not consume any animal products. That means no milk products, like cheese, yogurt, and ice cream, and no eggs from the animal. A vegan consumes only vegetables, fruits, whole grains, nuts, seeds, and oils. You may not know this, but Michael Zigomanis, a former forward on the Toronto Maple Leafs (#26) who currently plays for the team's minor-league affiliate, has been a vegetarian for four years and in 2011 he became a vegan. He is living proof that a vegetarian diet works for ice hockey players. A vegetarian youth ice hockey player can be just as strong and fast as a player who eats meat. To help you help your child, here is a list of animal- and plant-based protein sources.

Sources of Animal Protein

- Egg whites
- Whole eggs
- Cheddar cheese
- Milk

- Yogurt
- Cottage cheese
- Fish, pork, beef, chicken

Sources of Vegetarian/Plant Protein

- Nuts
- Seeds, (pumpkin and sunflower)
- Legumes (kidney beans, black beans, garbanzo beans, Navy beans, etc.)
- Tofu
- Quinoa***
- Soybeans***
- Nut butters

Vegetarian/plant sources of protein lack an amino acid. The grain group lacks isoleucine and lysine, and the legume family lacks methionine and tryptophan. But don't worry: When eaten together, like beans and rice, or a peanut butter and jelly sandwich, these food contain all 20 amino acids, just like the animal sources. The two foods labeled with three asterisks (***) are the exceptions. Soybeans, soybean products, and quinoa (a South American grain) are plant proteins that contain all 20 amino acids, making each of these foods a complete protein, just like meat. So when you eat tofu, or edamame, or a quinoa salad, or quinoa risotto, you are consuming the same amount of amino acids as you would if you ate a steak.

Why does this matter? And no, you don't have to remember the names of the amino acids. This is important because each protein molecule contains at least 20 amino acids linked together. This is called a complete protein. Non-animal sources of protein are sometimes referred to as incomplete, meaning lacking an amino acid.

Your child may begin to use the word "combining" or the phrase "complementary proteins." What this means is he is trying to consume food together in a meal to make sure he is eating a complete protein. Fear not! The human body is very smart. When your child eats a diet rich in fruits, vegetables, and whole grains the body will take care of building the needed proteins from the foods eaten.

You do need to worry about some vitamins and minerals. (I will mention them here, and you will learn more about them in the "Vitamins" and "Minerals" sections.) Vegans are at risk of not eating enough vitamin B-12. Why? Because this vitamin is only made from animal sources, with the exception of nutritional yeast, which can be purchased at a health food store and used to make recipes such as vegan mac and cheese.

If you buy Boca Burgers or Morningstar products (or any other brand), read the ingredient label and look for the word "cyanocobalamin." That is vitamin B-12. It may be listed as cobalamin. This will let you know that vitamin B-12 has been added to the product.

Vegans need to make sure they are eating enough foods rich in vitamin D (sunshine and cooked shiitake mushrooms), calcium (broccoli, spinach, black-eyed peas), zinc (white beans and, yes, chocolate), and iron (lentils, white beans, enriched flake cereal, and spinach). A lacto-ovo vegetarian is less likely to become deficient in these vitamins. The following list shows you the nutrients a vegetarian may not consume enough of and food sources to help you and your vegetarian hockey player make great choices.

> **Protein:** Meat contains protein consisting of all 20 amino acids. A vegetarian must combine fruits and vegetables with nuts, seeds, legumes (black beans, lentils, etc.), and grains to make complete proteins in the body. Soybeans and quinoa are two non-animal sources that contain all 20 amino acids just like meat.
>
> **Calcium:** Milk, yogurt, other dairy products. Vegetables: spinach, broccoli, carrots, green beans, and potatoes (all cooked). Calcium-fortified orange juice is an option.

Iron: Very important especially for vegetarian girls who need 26 mg/day once they reach puberty. Excellent sources: spinach, pinto beans, sunflower seeds, tofu, peanut butter, whole-wheat bread, oatmeal.

Zinc: Important for growth and development of children, brain functioning, and immune system. Boys need 8–11mg/day; girls need 8–9 mg/day. Whole-wheat bread, avocado, peanut butter, sunflower seeds, spinach, corn tortilla, spaghetti noodles.

Iodine: Needed to make thyroid hormones. Boys and girls need 120–150 mcg/day. Buy iodized salt.

Vitamin B-12: Used to make red blood cells. Non-fat milk, fortified, and cheddar cheese. This vitamin is only found in animal products with the exception of nutritional yeast.

Vitamin D: Important for bone health. Sunshine!! Milk, eggs, and some breads and orange juices that are fortified.

Omega 3 Fatty Acids: Memory, focus, heart health. Flax seeds, canola oil.

When people learn I am a dietitian, they ask me all kinds of questions. One common one is: "Can I eat too much protein?" Yes, too much protein is not going to help you or your child build more muscle. Too much protein can be damaging to your kidneys. This may happen if you use protein supplements. Granted, you would have to mega-dose for a long time, but I never recommend that my adult clients consume more than 1.8 grams of protein per kilogram of body weight (or 0.6–0.9 grams of protein per pound of body weight), and the amount depends on the sport. A child who fills himself up with too much animal protein may not be eating enough carbohydrates to provide lasting energy on the ice. And most importantly, too much animal protein can lead to a diet high in fat and saturated fats, which is not good for your heart or preventing certain cancers.

If you eat a wide variety of foods you will easily eat all the protein you need in a day, and possibly more. It is important to remember to choose lower-fat choices the majority of the time. Yes, rib-eye steaks can fit into the family meal plan, and so can fried chicken, but not every day. These fatty meats taste good, but as you will learn in Part II, these foods may not support speed on the ice.

Left Wing: Fat

Fat, the last member of the offensive lineup, provides your skater with 9 calories per gram. That may sound like a lot to you, but your skater needs these calories. Take a skater who weighs 110 pounds. Did you know he can burn 350 calories in an hour of practice? That is 525 calories burned in a 90-minute practice, and 700 calories in a two-hour practice.

You might be thinking, *Great, but I don't remember the last time I was able to burn 700 calories, and yes, I can pinch an inch.* Don't worry. That isn't the kind of fat I will be discussing. The fat discussed in this section is the fat you eat. That doesn't mean I just gave you a free pass to eat fried chicken every night. If you eat 2,000 calories a day, 20–35 percent, or 400–700 (45 g–78 g) calories, should come from fat.

There are so many low-fat products in the grocery store that you may feel fats are bad for you and should be avoided. Let me start by saying this: Fats are not the bad guy. Your body needs fat on it and in your diet. Yes, fat is essential for life, and it has many jobs to do.

Fat is your body's energy store. (You may want your store to be smaller, but your body will use that stored energy when it is needed.) The fat in your body performs the following jobs:

- Fats provide muscles with energy to work.

- Fat is your emergency supply of calories during a long illness.

- Fat acts like hockey pads on the inside of your body to protect your internal organs from shock.

- Fat is insulation against the cold; it is like a personal, built-in blanket.
- Fats are part of your cell membranes throughout your body.
- Fats are needed to make hormones, vitamin D, and bile.

The jobs of the fat in your food include the following:

- Fat provides essential fatty acids.
- Fat is rich in calories, providing 9 calories per gram.
- Fat helps your body absorb the fat-soluble vitamins A, D, E, and K. The food industry uses this fat property to sell salad dressing. Take a moment, grab a bottle of salad dressing out of your refrigerator, and read the words on the front. I bet it reads "aids in the absorption of fat-soluble vitamins."
- Fats make food taste and smell good.
- Fats make food tenderer. (Imagine a rib-eye steak without any marbled fat.)
- Fats in a meal make you feel full.
- Fats make you want to eat more by stimulating your appetite.

As you can see fats in your diet have many jobs, but all fats are not made the same. You consume three categories of fats in your diet: saturated fatty acids; unsaturated fatty acids, polyunsaturated fatty acids, and monounsaturated fatty acids; and trans fats.

Let me explain the differences.

- **Saturated** fats come from animals, and are solid at room temperature. Yes, butter is a saturated fat, and so is lard. Not too many people use lard in the family kitchen anymore, but you can still find it for sale in the grocery store. Some commercial bakers use it for pastries, like pie crusts. There are two plant sources that contain saturated fat: coconut and palm oil.

- **Unsaturated** fats come from plants and seeds, and these fats are liquid at room temperature. There are two subcategories in this category:
    o Polyunsaturated fats. These fats are the omega 6 fatty acids found in vegetable oils, corn, cottonseed, safflower, sesame, soybean, and sunflower oils, as well as seeds nuts and poultry fat; and the omega 3 fatty acids found in fish, fish oils, and flaxseeds. Omega 3s and omega 6s are essential to your diet, meaning you must get them from your food; your body can't make them.
    o Monounsaturated fats. These fats are the omega 3 fatty acids. These fats are found in fish, fish oil, walnuts, soybeans, and flax seeds. The cooking oils are olive, canola, and peanut oil.
- **Trans fats** are fats that are made in the lab. Trans fats are made from a fat that is naturally liquid at room temperature, and in the lab hydrogen atoms are added to the molecule (a process called hydrogenation), making it solid at room temperature (e.g., margarine).

Why do I need to make sure my child is eating enough fat and not too much?

Fat is needed for normal growth and development during your child's growing years. While you have heard a lot about low-fat diets, it is important to make sure your child is getting enough. It is recommended that children and teens between the ages of 4 and 18 years consume 25 to 35 percent of their daily intake from fat.

For example, if your child needs 2,500 calories a day, your child would need 625 calories to 875 calories each day from fat.

You can help your child by making sure you limit the amount of trans fats in his diet. Why? Trans fats have been shown to increase the bad cholesterol in your bloodstream (LDL) and decrease the good cholesterol (HDL) in your bloodstream.

Trans fats occur naturally in meats and dairy products, but these naturally occurring trans fats make up a small amount of what you eat. The majority of the trans fats that you eat come from prepackaged foods. You can find out how much you are eating by simply reading the label and looking for the phrase "partially hydrogenated." Trans fats are used by the food industry because they increase shelf life. Thus many cookies, cakes, canned frosting, crackers, and other treats may contain them, so read labels. The FDA required food companies to include trans fats on the food label in 2006. Since then many food companies have tried to reduce or eliminate the amount of trans fats in their products.

In my classes I teach my students that zero is only truly zero in a math class. Why? When the FDA mandated that food companies label their products with trans fats, it was determined that if a product contain 0.5 grams of trans fats per serving or less, the food company could place a 0 on the label for trans fats.

What does that for you and your family? Look for the term "partially hydrogenated" in the ingredients list on the food label. If a product lists the trans-fat grams as 0 yet the words "partially hydrogenated" are in the ingredients list, the product contains trans fats. Remember: If a product contains less than 0.5 grams of trans fat per serving, the company can legally list 0 for trans-fat grams. Is this horrible? It depends how often you eat the product. I use canned frosting in a pinch, and it does contain trans fats, but I use this type of frosting just a few times a year. Knowledge is power. You can buy the canned frosting or make your own. I encourage you to use this logic with all the prepackaged and prepared foods you buy.

Saturated fats are needed in your diet to ensure your body functions properly. All of the following functions in your body need saturated fat:

- Cell membranes
- Heart

- Liver
- Immune system
- Lungs
- Hormones
- Bones (to assimilate calcium, use calcium to build new bones)
- Genetic regulation
- Reducing hunger, satiety

That said, I am not recommending you load up on saturated fats, but I am saying you need to eat some.

Here is a list of the fats so you know how the fats you eat are categorized:

Saturated fats: milk, eggs, meats, cheese, butter, lard, coconut and palm oils

Polyunsaturated fats (omega 6 fatty acids): corn, vegetable, canola, safflower, sunflower oils

Monounsaturated fats (omega 3 fatty acids): olive oil, flax seeds, walnuts

Trans fats: many prepackaged foods (Read the ingredients list and look for the words "partially hydrogenated.")

At the beginning of this section I mentioned a daily fat intake of between 20 and 35 percent of the total calories consumed by you or your skater. To help you figure out where some of the fat is coming from when you eat packaged foods, I want to take you through a label-reading exercise I use in my classes.

Why? I find most people do not understand the difference between the DV% and the true fat % on food labels.

Take a look at the following label:

Nutrition Facts

Serving Size: 2 waffles (71g)

Amount Per Serving

Calories 190	Calories from Fat 45

	% Daily Value*
Total Fat 5g	8%
Saturated Fat 1g	5%
Trans Fat 0g	
Cholesterol 5 mg	2%
Sodium 450 mg	19%
Potassium	
Total Carbohydrate 32g	11%
Dietary Fiber 1 g	4%
Sugars 5 g	
Sugar Alcohols	
Protein 4 g	
Vitamin A 0 IU	0%
Vitamin C 0 mg	0%
Calcium 80 mg	8%
Iron 3.6 mg	20%

To determine the true percent fat per serving, use this equation:

Total calories from fat per servings ÷ total calories per serving.

Let's use the numbers from the food label. If you look at the top of the food label you will see calories per serving (190). Then straight across to the right you see calories from fat (45). Next you set up the equation to divide 45 by 190: 45/190 = .236. Now multiply by 100, which will give you the true percent fat per serving: .236 x 100 = 23.6% fat in two waffles.

Now look at the DV% column (8%). The DV% column represents the percentage of your daily fat intake that you would consume if you ate those two waffles. So each time you eat two waffles you are eating 8 percent of the total fat you need each day. It is important to remember that the DV% is not the percent fat per serving but the percentage of your required daily intake of fat.

Now it is time to apply all this fat knowledge to your player. Too much fat in a meal will certainly fill you up, but it may not give your hockey player the results you expect on the ice. Consider this true scenario:

Our Pee Wee team had traveled to South Carolina for the championship playoffs in 2012. We were so excited! If you have been in travel hockey for a while you know the craziness of these weekends. You spend the week before the trip organizing: "Do your skates still fit? Do your skates need to be sharpened? Did you talk to your teacher and make sure you know exactly what is happening the week after your hockey weekend? Where is your mouth guard?" The list goes on. Add to that making sure your player eats like a champion.

I witnessed firsthand a disaster during one game that weekend. Our team had a quick turnaround game, with less than two hours in between games. Most of our players remained at the rink and ate light foods: a sandwich, or some fruit, crackers, yogurt sticks (the typical snacks we pack for the team). Two players went out to eat with their families. That's all well and good, as family time is important during these weekends. However, it was clear when these two young men returned to the ice that their bodies were not fueled like champions.

I am not kidding you when I say I watched our two fastest skaters skate like they were wearing cinder blocks, not hockey skates!! The boys had eaten at a popular fast food restaurant and had not taken into account how quickly they would be getting back on the ice. Their choices greatly impacted their ability to play. (Thankfully the other skaters stepped up, and we won that game and the championship banner.)

Several years ago when my oldest son was a second-year Squirt I was the team manager and saw what happens to a team when the coach takes nutrition seriously and the players listen. We had an early-morning game—6 a.m. You know those mornings: Adrenaline is in the air for the hockey players, and all the parents are looking for coffee or dropping their player at the rink and taking coffee orders from the other parents before they hit the local Starbucks, Krispy Kreme, or Dunkin Donuts.

Well, the team won the playoff game. We were thrilled. Now the challenge: With little more than an hour turnaround before the championship game, we had to order out food. The coach asked my opinion. I told him one small breakfast burrito from McDonald's and one chocolate milk per player. We ordered enough for each player to have one of each plus the coaches. I will never forget when one of the players asked for a second burrito and the coach said, *"Only one!"* throwing his arms out to the side, as if he was yelling "safe" on the baseball field.

I understood his logic. He wanted his players fueled but not sluggish. And it worked. Our Squirt team, which had started with only five players the summer before the official season began, won the championship game and brought home the banner from the tournament weekend.

I wish every game would end like that one, and I know you feel the same way. To help you choose healthy fats for your child, consider adding lean meats, fish twice a week (my family likes tilapia and salmon), nuts for snacks, and milk and dairy products to your family's meal plan. When you cook these protein-rich foods, baking, broiling, roasting, poaching, sautéing, stir frying, and grilling are great methods that provide wonderful taste and not too much added fat, as is the case with deep frying.

Meet the Defensive Line: Vitamins and Minerals

Vitamins

Stop and think back to the moment that your child stated he wanted to play hockey. Do you remember that day? I do, and I was thrilled! I had been introduced to the sport by a student who played on our university team. I remember how much fun it was to watch my brother play and was happy my sons wanted to give it a try. I wasn't scared, though that all changed when I told a friend of mine. "Oh, that is such a dangerous sport" were the first words out of her mouth, followed by, "There are so many concussions in ice hockey. I wouldn't let my son play."

Can you relate? I see you smiling. Yes, ice hockey can be fraught with injury, but so can all the other sports children play. Heck, look at cheerleading. I am not so sure I would want my daughter "flying," but kids actively compete in cheerleading and love it! Just like hockey. Kids get cut, sprain ankles, pull muscles, and, unfortunately, break bones in all sports. Wouldn't it be great to know how to improve your skater's healing power with nutrition? In this section I will introduce vitamins to you and show you how you can use specific vitamins and foods to help with healing, when needed, and prevention.

What Are Vitamins?

Vitamins are micronutrients. These molecules are organic. They contain carbon, just like carbohydrates and proteins, but they do not provide any calories. Vitamins are needed in smaller amounts, thus the term "micronutrients."

Vitamins are calorie free and important for many functions in your body. Did you know some vitamins are needed to convert the food you eat into energy? Vitamins are catalysts; they help reactions take place. Your body can't make any vitamins, so you must obtain all the water-soluble and fat-soluble vitamins from your food. That is why they are referred to as essential nutrients. We must obtain these vitamins from the foods we eat.

Water-Soluble Vitamins

Vitamin C and the B vitamins are water soluble because they dissolve in water. These vitamins must be replaced daily. Remember: Your body is 60 percent water.

Vitamin C is also known as ascorbic acid, which means no-scurvy acid. Why? You may have heard British sailors referred to as limeys. This is because several hundreds of years ago sailors would die from scurvy, caused by a vitamin C deficiency they would suffer from on long sea voyages. Researchers in the late 1700s determined that just a small amount of lime juice would help more sailors survive. Every ship left port with a carton or more of limes for the voyage, after the connection was made among limes, vitamin C, and the prevention of scurvy.

Luckily we do not have to suffer from scurvy today. Vitamin C is important in the production of collagen in your body. Collagen is a protein that helps to glue your body together. It is important for your teeth, arteries, bones, skin, tendons, and cartilage. Now, I know you may be thinking, *Why do I need to know all this?* You may be surprised how important vitamin C is beyond "it will decrease the duration of a cold." Think about all the injuries in hockey. I know it is scary! But when injuries happen, you can help facilitate your skaters' healing with vitamin C. Vitamin C is crucial to help heal cuts, fractures, and broken bones. Vitamin C helps your body make collagen. If you are a seasoned hockey mom you have seen blood on the ice. That skater will need a hefty dose of vitamin C to make the scar that will "glue" the cut back together. When fractures and broken bones occur, vitamin C comes to the rescue by helping the bone to heal, too.

Hockey players are children first, and some children are picky eaters. You may wonder how to determine if your child is eating enough foods rich in vitamin C. If your child isn't eating enough fruits and vegetables, he may bruise easier, his cuts or bigger wounds will not heal as well, he may be more prone to pick up the cold virus at school, his gums may bleed, and his permanent teeth may become loose. These are just a few reasons to make sure your hockey player is getting the right amount of vitamin C for his age.

Now are you ready to load your refrigerator with vitamin C–rich fruits and vegetables? I know you are.

Fruits Rich in Vitamin C

- Avocado
- Oranges
- Clementines (tangerines; also sold by the name "Cuties")
- Strawberries
- Kiwi
- Papaya
- Guava

Vegetables Rich in Vitamin C

- Broccoli
- Bell peppers (green, red, yellow, and orange)
- Cauliflower
- Kale
- Brussels sprouts
- Mustard greens
- Spinach

Now that you know where to find good sources of vitamin C, make sure your player is getting enough every day. As your child grows from the ages of 4 to 13, his needs almost double from 25 mg/day to 45 mg/day. Your child can easily obtain this amount by eating at least three servings a day of the fruits and vegetables just listed. In this age range, boys and girls need the same amount of daily vitamin C. When your son reaches the ages of 14–18, he needs 75 mg/day and your daughter needs 65 mg/day. Your older skater will need to eat at least four to five servings of the foods listed.

I find if I keep my fruit on the countertop or easily available on a shelf in the refrigerator, my sons will grab fruit as a snack. I am not lying when I tell you my sons eat clementines like some children eat chips.

The B Vitamins: The Energizers

The B vitamins are water-soluble vitamins that are important for energy production. In other words, many of the B vitamins help convert the food we eat—protein, fat, and carbohydrates—to energy at the cellular level. Vitamin B12 is important for making red blood cells. It is fairly easy to make sure your hockey player is getting enough of these vitamins because B vitamins are found in most grain products, breads, and cereals.

Vitamin B1 (Thiamin), Vitamin B2 (Riboflavin), and Vitamin B3 (Niacin)

As a group these vitamins are important for your child's nerve and muscle action. Think about all those quick drills you watch your child practice. I know you want your skater's neurons firing at 100 percent in his brain, and the muscles in his body working at peak performance. These vitamins also help your child handle stress, be it on the ice or in the classroom. When it comes to getting enough B vitamins in your diet, it isn't hard; many of them travel together. The following foods are a good source of thiamin (B1), riboflavin (B2), and niacin (B3):

- Whole-wheat bread

- White bread, enriched
- Spaghetti noodles
- Corn tortillas
- Cooked spinach (excellent source of riboflavin)
- Peanut butter, chunky
- Sunflower seeds (excellent source of thiamin)
- Ground beef
- Chicken breast (excellent source of niacin)
- Canned tuna
- Hard-boiled eggs
- Broccoli
- Spinach

Children between the ages of 4 and 8 need 0.6 mg/day of thiamin and riboflavin, and 8 mg/day of niacin. As children grow, their needs increase. The following chart show daily amounts needed.

	Thiamin	Riboflavin	Niacin
Boys 9–13 yrs.	0.9 mg	0.9 mg	12 mg
Boys 14–18 yrs.	1.2 mg	1.3 mg	16 mg
Girls 9–13 yrs.	0.9 mg	0.9 mg	12 mg
Girls 14–18 yrs.	1.0 mg	1.0 mg	14 mg

Most children will consume the required amount by eating a variety of foods. For example, a child who eats 1 cup of fortified breakfast cereal with milk has already consumed his daily amount of niacin, and 50 percent of his riboflavin. Pack a whole-wheat chicken sandwich for lunch with milk, and your skater is well on his way to consuming his daily requirement of all three of these B vitamins.

Vitamin B5 (Pantothenic Acid)

This vitamin is found in a wide variety of foods, and deficiencies are rare. Pantothenic acid helps your hockey player use carbohydrates for energy. Like vitamin C, pantothenic acid wards off infection and helps to keep your hockey player's blood sugar stable. Children between the ages of 4 and 8 need 3 mg/day. Boys and girls between the ages of 9 and 13 need 4 mg/day, and between the ages of 14 and 18 need 5 mg/day.

Foods rich in this vitamin include:

- Meat, fish, poultry
- Mushrooms
- Beans
- Whole-grain products and fortified grain products

A breakfast of 1 cup fortified breakfast cereal is enough to help all of these children meet their daily requirement. Young children would only need ½ cup of cereal. For older children, tweens, and teens, 1 cup of sautéed mushrooms with steak or chicken provides the daily requirement. For vegetarian hockey players, 1 cup of sautéed mushrooms is loaded with all the pantothenic acid needed for the day.

Vitamin B6 (Pyridoxine)

Vitamin B6 helps the muscle cells to use the stored glycogen as glucose. In other words, vitamin B6 is like the man who shoveled the coal on an old steam engine train; no coal, and the train will not get up the mountain. If your muscles can't convert the stored glycogen to glucose, your feet will not get across the finish line. Excellent sources of pyridoxine are cooked spinach, garbanzo beans, and chicken breasts.

Other sources include whole-wheat bread, corn tortillas, broccoli, green beans, oranges, avocados, pinto beans, chunky peanut butter, sunflower seeds, and canned tuna.

Children between the ages of 4 and 8 need 0.6 mg/day. Boys and girls between the ages of 9 and 13 need 1.0 mg/day, boys between the ages of 14 and 18 need 1.3 mg/day, and girls between the ages of 14 and 18 need 1.2 mg/day.

One cup of breakfast cereal contains 2.0 mg of vitamin B6. If you skater ate a banana before practice he would be consuming close to 50 percent of his needed vitamin B6.

Folate (Folic Acid)

I know you are familiar with folic acid, also known as folate, because you were pregnant. Folic acid is the vitamin that helps prevent neural tube defects, such as spina bifida. In addition folic acid aids in the making of DNA and red blood cells in your body. Red blood cells are important because these cells help to carry iron and oxygen throughout your body. If your child has ever been diagnosed with anemia, he might not have been eating foods rich in folic acid. Anemia will keep your hockey player from playing at his best. A tired hockey player will not score any goals or be able to intercept the puck from an opposing team's player speeding toward the net he is trying to defend.

To ensure your hockey player consumes enough folic acid, make sure he is eating foods rich in folate. Great sources of folate include leafy green vegetables, like kale and spinach, and legumes, like pinto beans, black beans, kidney beans, and peanuts.

Children between the ages of 4 and 8 need 200 mcg/day. Boys and girls between the ages of 9 and 13 need 300 mcg/day, and 400 mcg/day are needed for boys and girls between the ages of 14 and 18.

If your skater likes lentil soup, great—1 cup provides them with more than 300 mcg. And once again, fortified breakfast cereal tops the list with 600 mcg in a ¾-cup serving.

Vitamin B12 (Cobalamin)

If your child is a vegetarian you should pay close attention to foods rich in vitamin B12. This vitamin is only found in animal products, with the exception of nutritional yeast. If your child is a lacto-ovo vegetarian, all dairy and egg products contain vitamin B12. But if your child is a vegan, you will want to become familiar with the term "cyanocobalamin." This is the form of vitamin B12 that is added to products such a MorningStar's spicy black bean burgers (a personal favorite). A deficiency in this vitamin can cause a type of anemia—not what you want for your active player.

Children between the ages of 4 and 8 need 1.2 mcg/day. Boys and girls between the ages of 9 and 13 need 1.8 mcg/day, and those between the ages of 14 and 18 need 2.4 mcg/day.

Clams are an excellent source of vitamin B12, so if your hockey player loves New England clam chowder, that's great. Baked salmon for dinner would be fantastic for the entire family because everyone would get the required amount of B12, not to mention the great omega 3 fatty acids.

Biotin and Pantothenic Acid

These two B vitamins aid in the conversion of food into energy like thiamin, riboflavin, and niacin. Biotin and pantothenic acid are found in many foods, and deficiencies are rarely diagnosed in individuals eating a well-balanced diet.

Fat-Soluble Vitamins

Fat-soluble vitamins are the second class of vitamins. These vitamins are stored and used in the liver and fatty tissue of your body. Because vitamins A, D, E, and K are soluble fat, you do not need to replenish these daily, and if taken in excess can become toxic.

Vitamin A

Vitamin A is known for helping you see at night when you are driving home from hockey practice. You may have heard if you eat a carrot a day it will help you with your night vision. Vitamin A is found in two different forms. The plant form of vitamin A is known as beta carotene; this form is not toxic. Beta carotene is used by your body to make three different forms of vitamin A. This form of the vitamin A functions as an antioxidant.

Choose fruits and vegetables that are orange or yellow in color. One vegetable rich in vitamin A that may surprise you is spinach. One cup of cooked spinach contains more vitamin A in the form of beta carotene than 1 cup of cooked carrots. So you can't always rely on the color rule. The other form of vitamin A is found in the livers of animals; thus animal products contain this type of vitamin A.

Vitamin A not only helps with night vision, but it helps keep our skin cells healthy, on the inside and outside of our body, and helps keep our immune system healthy.

However, you can have too much of a good thing, and vitamin A can be toxic if you are eating a lot of animal products and taking a supplement.

What happens if my child eats too many carrots? Here is a true story that I hear time and time again: Imagine your former junk food junkie suddenly decides to "get healthy" for the upcoming hockey season. In doing so, he starts to choose baby carrots over potato chips. You are thrilled—until one day you look at your child and notice a strange orange color on his palms. No, this isn't paint. He has overdosed on carrots, and his orange-pigmented palms are a warning sign to lay off the carrots for a while. His palms will return to their natural color. And remember: Beta carotene is not toxic, so don't worry. He will be fine.

Here is a quick list of RDAs for Vitamin A. Retinol equivalents are in parentheses.

- Boys and girls 4–8 years need 400 mcg/day (1,333 IU).

- Boys and girls 9–13 years need 600 mcg/day (2,000 IU).

- Boys 14–18 years need 900 mcg/day (3,000 IU).

- Girls 14–18 years need 700 mcg/day (2,333 IU).

If your child likes sweet potatoes, spinach, kale, carrots, and red peppers, that is great. If he does not like any of those foods, fortified breakfast cereal will provide him with a good start.

Vitamin D

Vitamin D is needed for strong bones. When you go for your run, your body is making vitamin D from the sun. When your child plays outside, he is absorbing vitamin D from the sun. Unfortunately when you spend time inside, which you know is the case for hockey practices and games, your child doesn't get the sunshine he needs. In addition to getting sunshine, make sure you child is drinking fortified milk, and eating salmon, sardines, or mackerel.

If your son is like mine, when he eats fish he will choose salmon. The amount of vitamin D needed is the same for everyone younger than 50: 200 IU (5 mcg). If you or your child is ever found to be deficient in vitamin D your doctor will prescribe a higher-dose vitamin D supplement for you to take during a set amount of time. This is safe under a doctor's supervision.

When it comes to getting your vitamin D from the sun, where you live makes a big difference. If you live in the Boston area or further north, there are times in the winter months when you will not be able to get enough of the UVB rays to make vitamin D. Fear not: Your vitamin D is stored in your liver and the stored amount is usually enough to last all year, so do not worry about the winter months. Make sure that during the sunny months in spring, summer, and fall that you get at least 10 minutes of sun on your arms or face, three times a week, between 11 a.m. and 2 p.m. Consider this your vitamin D savings bank for the winter.

If you have a friend who has darker skin, she will need more time in the sun, and so will her hockey player. Their skin is more protected from the UVB rays and it takes longer for their body to make vitamin D.

Vitamin E

Vitamin E is known as an antioxidant. It helps your body fight off the damaging effects caused by free radicals. Yes, I know that sounds like science gobble-gook. Have you ever rubbed oil on a frying pan before putting it away? You may have done this because you saw your mother or grandmother do it, but the real reason you do this is to prevent rusting. Rusting on a frying pan is oxidative damage. Oxidative damage in your body is caused by free radicals. Vitamin E–rich foods like avocados, spinach, and sunflower seeds help to fight disease, cancer, and aging caused by free radical damage in your body.

Vitamin E is non-toxic; you will not build up a toxic level in your body.

Nuts and seeds are excellent sources of vitamin E. Sunflower seeds and almonds can be mixed with raisins, dried fruit (cranberries, cherries, blueberries), and semisweet chocolate mini chips to make a yummy, energizing trail mix.

Vitamin K

Vitamin K is important for blood clotting. For your hockey player, vitamin C, which helps with collagen formation for the scar, and vitamin K, for clotting, are two very important vitamins.

The spinach you put in your smoothie this morning is a great source of vitamin K. But did you know the bacteria in your large intestine make another form of vitamin K? That is why every one of your children received a vitamin K drop just after birth. When children are born their little large intestines were void of any bacteria. They need that drop of vitamin K to help kick-start their body's production of this important vitamin. Now they are strong, fast hockey players, and you need to make sure they are eating vitamin K–rich foods such as Brussels sprouts (we call them little cabbage heads in my house), broccoli, leafy green vegetables (collards, cress, spinach, turnip greens, mustard greens, beet greens, Swiss chard, broccoli rabe, radicchio), and finally lettuce, asparagus, and cabbage.

Should My Child Take Vitamin Supplements?

It is always best to feed your child a well-rounded diet. That way your child will obtain the vitamins that they need. I give my sons a multivitamin formulated specifically for children each day. I do this because I feel like it gives them a small amount of protection on the days when their appetites are poor. I never buy a vitamin that contains iron. (I will discuss iron in the minerals section. However, it is important to note here that children can become toxic from iron.) Read the labels on the vitamins and make sure your children consume a variety of foods. Remember: It is important not to use a supplement as a crutch and in place of food.

Minerals

The mere mention of minerals may give you flashbacks to college chemistry, or you may smile thinking of all the gold jewelry you love. However, I am going to introduce you to all the minerals that are important for your skater's body. Think about the upcoming season. Your skater will need great focus and energy as his athletic demands increase, as does the work to maintain a good GPA to remain on the team. Minerals found in the foods your skater eats have many important jobs to fulfill in his body: carrying oxygen in the blood to help with energy and mental focus, healing, growth, fluid balance, prevention of muscle cramps, and more.

You know the feeling: You are only two months into the new season, and your child's skates, hockey pants, and chest protector are too small! That's right: Your child is growing! Now stop and think about it. Growing bones *must* remain strong. This is why learning about the minerals is so important. Strong bones are so important to all children in every sport, and when you add fast skating and the possibility of being checked, you want your hockey player to have a good, strong skeleton. There are a total of 14 minerals that work wonders in your body without you lifting a finger. Imagine if you had 14 helpers around the house, how easy it would be to keep it cleaned and organized. Okay, the minerals don't clean your body, but they are involved in hundreds of jobs, day in and day out, that we rarely notice. I like to refer to these minerals as your silent heroes.

Let's start with the magnificent seven: calcium, phosphorous, magnesium, potassium, sulfur, sodium, and chloride. Your body requires large amounts of these minerals every day; that is why you may know them as the major minerals.

Your skater is growing, every night. That is correct. It isn't your imagination. Your child begins each new day taller, and his body contains more cells than when he went to bed the night before. That has always amazed me. I know, as a mom, that one of your biggest fears is injury on the ice. From the bruises or cuts, to the laceration that needs stitches, to sprains, strains, fractures, or concussions, you hold your breath, maybe even say a prayer, and watch your hockey player take the ice. There is no denying hockey is a fast sport, and injuries happen. In this section you will learn about the different major and trace minerals, and why these minerals are important to your child's health. I will begin with the most familiar mineral: calcium.

Calcium

Take a look around the children entering school on any given day. Do you see any of them on crutches? Many children break bones playing sports; sometimes it seems to be a rite of passage as a child to get your cast signed. Some breaks are unavoidable, but you can increase the chance that your child doesn't have to suffer from a broken bone by teaching him what to eat and drink. I loved Tab (yes, I am a child of the '70s), and I drank it daily in my late teens and early 20s, not knowing what I was doing to my body. Did you know all dark sodas contain phosphoric acid? It doesn't matter if the soda is diet or regular; these beverages do not support bone growth. Coke, Pepsi, Dr. Pepper—all contain phosphoric acid, which has been linked to lower bone density in some studies.

A 1994 Harvard study found a strong correlation between cola consumption and fractures in teenage girls. When you or your child drinks a dark soda the blood in his body becomes more acidic. The body doesn't want acidic blood, so calcium leaves the bone (that's right, your skeleton) to help the blood maintain its preferred pH. In addition, phosphoric acid can cause digestive problems because it neutralizes the acid in the stomach. Your child needs acid in the stomach; the protein he eats to grow his skating muscles is broken down for digestion with the help of the stomach acid. And one last point: It takes just 20 minutes for the acid to start dissolving the enamel on your child's teeth (according to an Ohio Dental Association press release). Scary, isn't it? I bet you are asking yourself, *Do you still let your sons drink dark soda?* Yes. I buy sodas on special occasions and holidays, and I buy the ones in the bottle. My boys love the "old-fashioned" Coke and they drink less, because these bottles contain fewer fluid ounces than the cans. Coke, Pepsi, and yes, Twinkies are a part of childhood, but not every day.

Calcium is needed for strong bones and teeth. Some children, especially boys, will continue to add inches to their height even once they leave for college. I have had college basketball players share in class that they grew 6 inches after high school. Young adults up to the age of 30 continue to build bone. You are teaching your child lifelong habits. I know you want your hockey player to be strong. A strong skeleton will enable him to continue playing hockey in college, be it club or varsity, and maybe the NHL. Not to mention, calcium is needed for proper muscle contraction and blood clotting. Calcium is crucial for healthy bones, teeth, and muscles.

As your child grows from 4 to 18 years old, his daily needs increase from 800 mg/day to 1,300 mg/day. Some choices to consider are almonds, milk, yogurt, kale, tofu, cheddar cheese, spinach, pinto beans, and corn tortillas. Sesame seeds are a great source of calcium and can be added to a homemade trail mix to add to a lunch. Many milks, such as soy milk, rice milk, and almond milk, are good sources of calcium. Calcium is even added to breads and orange juices. Three to four servings day of these foods will help your child consume enough calcium.

One last note: Try to limit the fast food and prepackaged foods you and your child consume. The excess salt in the diet can cause calcium to be lost from the bones.

Phosphorous

Phosphorous is calcium's teammate in building strong bones. This mineral is needed by all of the cells in your body. You may have heard of the substance "creatine phosphate." This is the first energy system used by your child's body when he bursts onto the ice for his shift.

Creatine phosphate is used to produce very quick energy, in the first few seconds of activity. As your child grows his needs for phosphorous increase from 500 mg/day to 1,250 mg/day. Some good choices include corn tortillas, milk, peanut butter, and ground beef. Children 4 to 8 years of age need 500 mg/day; a cheeseburger and a glass of milk, or pinto beans and cheese rolled up in a corn tortilla with a glass of milk would provide the necessary phosphorus for the day. Adolescents aged 14 to 18 need 1,250 mg/day. A chopped chicken breast on a bed of fresh spinach, sprinkled with sunflower seeds and grated cheese, and a glass of milk would provide more than half of the daily amount needed.

To put your mind at ease, toxicities and deficiencies are rare.

Magnesium

Magnesium is the third major mineral that is important for building strong bones. Like calcium, magnesium is important in muscle contraction. Your skater's needs will increase from 130 to 410 mg/day between the ages of 4 and 18; teenage girls need 360 mg/day and teenage boys need 410 mg/day. Sunflower seeds, peanut butter, and spinach are excellent choices. If your child likes sandwiches and homemade French toast, use whole-wheat bread. Why? The amount of magnesium is greatly reduced when whole-wheat flour is refined into enriched white flour. Two slices of whole-wheat bread contain 126 mg, and two slices of enriched bread contain only 22 mg. If you give your child a vitamin, remember to keep the vitamins out of reach and do not exceed the dosage. Too much, usually in supplement form, can cause diarrhea. Magnesium deficiencies are rare.

Potassium

If you have ever complained about muscle cramps to your running buddies, they may have asked you if you were eating enough potassium-rich foods. And they would have been correct. Potassium is the major mineral that helps to decrease cramping. It can be found in broccoli, bananas, spinach, ground beef, and peanut butter, to name a few foods. To ensure your child is eating enough potassium-rich foods, encourage foods in their natural state. Bananas (100 g, about an average size banana) contain 358 mg of potassium and only 1 mg of sodium. One and half cups of broccoli florets contain 293 mg of potassium and 41 mg of sodium, and two slices of white bread contain 131 mg of potassium and 592 mg sodium. You can see the more processed a food is, the less potassium it contains, and the more sodium.

Sulfur

This mineral may smell bad, like a rotten egg, but it is so important for your body. It is part of the super antioxidant glutathione. Remember: Antioxidants help to fight off infections. Sulfur is also important for energy production. Foods like garlic, onions, cabbage, and Brussels sprouts contain the sulfur-containing amino acids methionine and cysteine. An intake amount has not been established, nor has a toxic amount.

Sodium

Sodium is easily found in the diets of many adults and children. It helps to maintain blood pressure and fluid balance, and aids in muscle contraction and firing of the nerves in your body. Believe it or not, the salt shaker is not guilty when it comes to added salt. Three-quarters of the salt you eat comes from processed foods. You and your children only need 1–1.5 g of sodium a day. That is 1,000mg–1,500 mg/day.

Do an experiment. The next time you eat at a fast-food restaurant or even a sit-down restaurant, look at the nutrient facts sheets. You will be shocked. Your child can consume more than half of the recommended amount of sodium with one meal choice. Yes, sodium is important, but remember that too much will work against your body in many ways. Children can be diagnosed with high blood pressure. Seventy-five percent of the sodium we eat comes from processed foods. Read the labels on some of the foods you wouldn't expect—like bread. The scary truth is that most of the time we can't taste this hidden salt. True story: I taught a young man who had been on blood pressure medicine since he was 14 (!). I met him at age 19.

He was a student in the nutrition class I teach at East Carolina University, and during my class he made many dietary changes and increased his exercise. A year later I ran into him and he said, "Mrs. Lukhard, I am not on any medications!" That was music to my ears.

Chloride

Table salt is where you will find the chloride in your diet and your child's diet. Table salt is 40 percent sodium and 60 percent chloride by weight. It is an essential nutrient, which means you need to get it from your diet; your body can't make it. The acid in your stomach, hydrochloric acid, which is responsible for helping you digest that steak you ate, is made with chloride. We need 750 mg/day. If you or your child eats too much processed food you could be eating too much sodium and chloride. Remember: A fruit bowl on the countertop is easy to reach and in sight, so your children will think to reach for fruit. And just like with sodium, too much chloride can cause you or your child's blood pressure to increase.

Trace Minerals

Trace minerals are minerals that are essential to your body, but you need them in much smaller amounts so they are called the trace minerals. These minerals help carry oxygen throughout out your body, help your body grow, heal your wounds, make collagen, aid in the production of your thyroid hormone, and function as an antioxidant. These minerals are as equally important as the major minerals.

Iron

Iron is needed by your body to carry oxygen in the blood and to store oxygen in your muscles. Iron is needed for healing, proper immune function, and collagen production. Hemoglobin is the protein in red blood cells, and iron is part of the heme compound that makes up hemoglobin. Myoglobin is a protein that also contains heme, and myoglobin is found in your muscles.

Many foods contain iron. You may be thinking of red meat, and you would be correct, but non-animal sources are also good sources of iron. I will set your mind at ease right now: If your hockey player has come to you and said he wants to become a vegetarian, fear not: After you finish this section you will be armed with information to help you and your child.

Heme iron is found in animal sources, and your body easily absorbs this type of iron. Non-heme iron is found in non-animal sources such as cooked spinach, which contains 3 mg of iron in ½ cup cooked; whole-wheat bread; oatmeal; green beans; enriched pasta, of which 1 cup cooked contains 2 mg; and sunflower seeds. When you eat non-heme sources of iron, add a vitamin C–rich food and you will increase the amount of iron that your body absorbs. For example, if you have pasta, spinach, and feta cheese for lunch, add a side of fresh strawberries. Your body will absorb more of the non-heme iron in this meal.

When boys are girls are young, 4 to 8 years of age, they need 10 mg of iron each day. This could be accomplished by eating fortified cereal for breakfast. Meat, poultry, raisins, and pasta all contain iron. Children ages 9 to 13 need 8 mg/day, boys ages 14 to 18 need 11 mg/day, and girls ages 14 to 18 need 15 mg/day. (If she is a vegetarian, she will need 26 mg/day.) Please note that many multivitamins contain 15–18 mg of iron; please read the labels before purchasing. I always choose a multivitamin that contains 6 mg or less of iron. Iron toxicity is a reason many children are hospitalized each year. Vitamin supplements look like candy and treats. When my sons were much younger, I told them, "Only Mommy gives you these." I kept them out of reach, which needed to be pretty high; they were good climbers.

Zinc

Zinc is considered the growth mineral. When children are deficient in zinc (usually seen in developing countries) they do not grow tall or increase in weight when compared to children who are not deficient in zinc. Sources of zinc include meat, fish, poultry, whole grains, and Brazil nuts.

Copper

Copper is needed for energy production, to make collagen, as an antioxidant, and to transport iron. A deficiency can lead to anemia, and toxicities are rare. Children ages 4 to 8 need 440 mcg/day, and the amount increases to 890 mcg/day by the time they are between the ages of 14 and 18. Some sources include nuts and seeds, avocados, and green leafy vegetables like spinach.

Iodine

Iodine is needed so your body can make thyroid hormones, which are important to your metabolism. When you buy salt make sure you are buying iodized salt, unless you have been told by your doctor or your child's pediatrician not to. Iodized salt has greatly eliminated iodine deficiencies, which are very harmful to a growing fetus's brain. As your child grows his needs will increase from 90 mcg/day for ages 4 to 8, to 120 mcg/day for ages 14 to 18. There is no difference in the daily amount needed for your sons or daughters. In addition to iodized salt your child will get iodine in his diet from seafood or seaweed-wrapped food like sushi.

Selenium

In the "Vitamins" section you learned about antioxidants and the importance of those vitamins in disease prevention. Selenium is a mineral that acts as an antioxidant. It is also needed for thyroid function. You need it in very small amounts. Children need 30–55 mcg as they grow from age 4 to age 18. Some food choices include whole-wheat bread, spaghetti noodles, ground beef, sunflower seeds, eggs, and tuna (an excellent source). Since the amount needed in your child's diet is much lower than the toxic level of 1,000 mcg (reached by supplementing), I would not worry about toxicity.

Chromium

Chromium helps insulin move the sugar in your bloodstream into your cells so energy can be made. This is especially important to your hockey player. Your skater needs the sugar in his cells to enable energy to be produced during practices and games. Children ages 4 to 8 need 15 mcg/day, boys ages 9 to 13 need 25 mcg/day, girls ages 9 to 13 need 21 mcg/day, adolescent boys ages 14 to 18 need 35 mcg/day, and girls ages 14 to 18 need 25 mcg/day. Good food choices include whole-grain products, broccoli, green beans, grape juice, and spices. To increase the amount of chromium absorbed by the body, add 100 mg of vitamin C to your day by adding an orange and 1 cup of broccoli.

Manganese

Manganese is important to a hockey player because it helps with healing cuts by aiding in the body's production of collagen to make the scar that glues the cut together. It also helps the body make glucose for energy when carbohydrates are not available. (I hope this is never the case for your player.) Manganese is needed in very small amounts, and if your child eats vegetables, whole grains, peanut butter, and leafy greens he will consume the 1.5 mg/day needed for 4- to 8-year-olds, 1.9 mg/day for 9- to 13-year-old boys, 1.6 mg/day for 9- to 13-year-old girls, 2.2 mg/day for 14- to 18-year-old boys, and 1.6 mg/day for 14- to 18-year-old girls. (Note: These are adequate intakes, not RDAs because the food and nutrition board of the Institute of Medicine does not have enough information on this mineral to determine a recommended daily allowance.)

Electrolytes

I know you have heard this sentence as you greet your child after practice with his sweat-soaked head, and red and sweaty face: "Mom, can I have a Gatorade?" Like most moms you probably agreed. Your hockey player has skated his legs off for the past hour and a half, and he looks like he stepped out of a shower. When you kiss his cheek, you can taste the salt. Sports drinks help to replace the lost electrolytes: potassium, sodium, and chloride. You have just learned about these minerals in the major mineral section, but I wanted to highlight them. These minerals need to be replaced after a long practice, lasting more than an hour.

I have given you a ton of information in this section, so to summarize I hope you remember this: All foods in their natural state are going to contain more minerals and less sodium than processed foods. These minerals help your skater to play his best. Foods rich in iron will help you're your skater think fast on the ice and in the classroom. Foods rich in calcium, magnesium, and phosphorus will make his bones stronger. The electrolytes will help your skater's body recover after a long practice or game.

Part II: Let the Game Begin

Get ready.
Now you will learn how to apply all of the information you read in Part I.

Step 2

Water: How to Calculate Your Skater's Needs

In Part I you learned about the importance of water, and I hope you are beginning to see how easy it is to make sure your skater is well hydrated—and the consequences if he is not. I can hear you asking me, *Kim, how do I know how much water/fluid to give him before practice or a game?* It isn't complicated. Actually it is quite simple. Follow the "fluid prescription" that follows and your child will have the focus, legs, and memory needed to get through a great practice, and not to mention, no headache (that is, unless it is truly time for a new helmet).

The fluid prescription starts during the school day. If your child isn't drinking enough water during the day, remind him to take sips from the water fountain every chance he gets. I was thrilled when I visited my 12-year-old son's class last year and saw water bottles on the desks. This way you know the children are reminding themselves they need to drink. It is hard to ignore a bottle of water.

How do you know if your child is drinking enough water? Use the pee test. It is as simple as teaching your child to look at the color of his urine. Dark yellow = dehydrated. Your child could easily cramp during practice or a game. Ideally you want the urine to be light yellow or close to clear. Then you know your child is well hydrated and should continue to drink the amount he needs for the day. Your child can use this test during the school day, especially if he is not allowed to have a water bottle at his desk. The pee test will help him remember to get a drink at the water fountain, and this will help him stay hydrated during school.

Regardless of when your child's practice is scheduled, use the following guidelines to help him be well hydrated.

2 hours before practice or a game: 2 cups

10–20 minutes before taking the ice: 1 cup

During the practice or game: a quick sip after each shift

You can get more specific by using the following equation for your player, based on weight. When your child is getting ready for practice or a game, make a bottle of water based on one hour of ice time. Your child needs 13 ml/kg/hour. He should have the water bottle with him on the bench (or above the net if he is a goalie) and drink when he needs to. This translates like this:

- My son is 92 pounds. (Convert to kilograms by dividing the weight in pounds by 2.2.)
- 42 kg x 13 ml =546 ml for an hour of skating
- That translates to a little over 2 cups, or about 17 ounces.
- The water bottle he uses holds 24 ounces, so I know he is covered for a practice lasting just an hour. If his practice is 90 minutes or two hours, I multiply the 546 ml x 1.5 ml = 819 ml, or 3.2 cups or 26 ounces; for two hours 546 ml x 2 =1,092 ml, or 4.3 cups or 35 ounces.
- This equation will ensure your player is well hydrated.

Rehydrating after a practice or a game is important, too. To determine how much your child needs to replenish after he gets off the ice, multiply his weight in kilograms x 4 ml x the number of hours exercised:

- 42 kg x 4 ml x 2 = 336 ml or 11 ounces for a two-hour practice

I encourage you to watch the coaches. Sometimes they are so focused on the practice or game they do not think to remind the players to drink. This is important at all ages!!

A word about sports drinks: Water is a must during practice. Sports drinks provide some carbohydrates, but these drinks may cause gastric distress in some players. The sports drinks on the market are formulated for an athlete who weighs 175 pounds. My sons use a sports drink that is specially formulated for youth athletes made by INFINIT Nutrition. The product is called :2-D1. It has less sugar and no high-fructose corn syrup. (For more information about this product visit **www.InfinitNutrition.com**. If you use my code, *hockeymomrd,* you will receive a 10% discount when you order.)

Step 3
Carbohydrates: How to Choose the Best Energy Foods

You learned about carbohydrates in Part I. Now let me show you how to apply the information.

To ensure your youth hockey player has great choices when you are stuck at a rink with a quick turnaround time, I have created a chart for you to use. Our locker room is usually stocked with the following: bananas, apples, grapes, crackers (peanut butter and cheese filled), yogurt sticks, bagels (cinnamon raisin is a favorite), Gatorade, and water.

½ hour to 1 hour before practice	Light snack: 15–30 g carbohydrates, very little fat	A banana, 17 grapes, pretzels, low-fiber cereal (e.g., Honey Nut Cheerios)
2–4 hours before practice	Light meal: 30–40 g carbohydrate, limited fat, moderate protein	A turkey, ham, or chicken sandwich, pretzels, a drink (no soda), and fruit
4–5 hours before practice	Big meal: 50–60 g carbohydrates, moderate protein and fat	A baked or roasted meat with potatoes, bread, fruit, and fluids OR pasta with red or cream sauce, bread, fruit, and fluids

Make sure your skater also packs a light snack for just before ice time.

Don't let this confuse you. The following table will help you determine how many carbohydrates are in specific foods. These are average amounts of carbohydrates per serving; some products, like breads, may vary. When in doubt, read the label!

Food	Serving Size	Carbs/Serving Size
Bread, white or whole wheat	1 slice	15 grams
Cinnamon raisin bagel	½ bagel	15 grams
Banana	½ banana	15 grams
Grapes	17 grapes	15 grams
Yogurt stick (Yoplait)	1 tube/stick	13 grams
Crackers (saltines, peanut butter and cheese crackers)	6 saltines	15 grams
Apples	1 small	15 grams
Gatorade	8 ounces	14 grams

Fiber

Fiber is important for your skater's digestive health. But keep in mind that too much fiber before ice time may cause stomach cramps.

Boys and girls need fiber daily just like adults, but they need less. Adults need 25 grams to 35 grams daily. Children need their age plus 5 in grams of daily fiber. For example, my 10-year-old son needs 15 grams of fiber daily. I have listed some high-fiber foods here.

The following vegetables contain 3 grams per ½-cup cooked or 1 cup raw:

- Brussels sprouts
- Carrots
- All colors of bell peppers

- Legumes are an excellent source of fiber. All contain about 7 grams of fiber per ½ cup:
    - Black beans, pinto beans, lentils, split peas
    - Garbanzo beans (the base for hummus)
- The following fruits contain 3 grams of fiber per serving:
    - Apricots (4 whole, 8 halves dried)
    - Blackberries (¾ cup)
    - Raspberries (¾ cup)
    - Strawberries (1¼ cup)
    - Tangerines (2 small)

Step 4

Protein: Eat for Skating Power

By now you know how important protein is, and you are probably thinking, *How can I make sure my child is getting enough protein?* First, it is important to remember that no children are alike, and their nutrition needs are as unique as the color of their eyes and skin, and whether they have freckles or not. When it comes to determining the amount of protein your child needs you must do some math. Stay with me; I am taking you back to fourth-grade math class. (I promise I will keep it short and sweet.)

First, you must convert your child's weight in pounds (lb) to weight in kilograms (kg).

Divide your child's pounds by 2.2.
Why? There are 2.2 lbs in each kilogram of weight.

I will use my son as an example. Right now he is 12 years old and weighs 92 pounds. To determine how much he needs use either of these formulas during the season:

>weight in pounds x 0.6 g – 0.9 g (to get a range)
>using metric measures: kg x 1.3 g – 2.0 g

Example:
>92 lbs, so he needs 55 g – 83 g
>or 42 kg x 1.3 – 2.0 = 55 g – 84 g

During the off-season players need less, unless they are playing another sport.
Your child needs protein to grow to their full potential. Your child can get all the protein he needs by eating a variety of foods. When you think of protein I am sure that meat, fish, chicken, turkey, and eggs come into your mind first. But many foods contain protein: lentil

soup, hummus, refried beans, black beans, and cottage cheese, just to name a few.
Here are some ideas for meals for your youth ice hockey player:

- The childhood classic: peanut butter and jelly on whole-wheat bread
- Tortillas with beans and cheese
- Guacamole and whole-wheat pita chips
- Spaghetti and red sauce
- Manicotti
- Quinoa risotto
- Vegetarian lasagna
- Greek pizza, with white cheese and spinach

A quick look at regular foods can show you that it is very easy for your child to obtain all the protein he needs from foods:

Let's look at my 92-pound son again. He needs 55–84 grams of protein daily during the hockey season.

Here are some of his favorite foods:

1 c. milk (8 g) x 3 cups a day = 24 g

2 T. peanut butter (7 g) x 2 servings a day = 14 g

Chickpeas (1/2 c. = 7 g) cooked with spinach (1/2 c. = 3 g), garlic, and onions a 1-cup serving = 10 g

Banana = 1 g

1 egg = 6 g

Spaghetti with tomato sauce: 1 cup = 8g

Tilapia fish: 3 oz. = 22 g; 5 oz. = 35 g

All of these foods add up to 98 g of protein, more than what my son needs in a day. It isn't difficult to eat real food and obtain all the protein needed and more.

Step 5

Road Trip

A travel weekend is fast approaching. Traveling is part of playing ice hockey. Think back to the last time you took a long family trip, either in the car or on a plane. Remember the excitement that built up to the weekend? Now, remember how your skin felt. I love traveling with my sons, and I take tons of extra moisturizing lotions and drink tons of water once we arrive at our hotel.

Why? Traveling by plane and car can be dehydrating to your body. The first item you should think of is water. You can pack individual bottles or jugs of water, and cups for the car. If traveling by plane, you will be more restricted by travel rules. The most important thing to remember when traveling is that you want your player fueled and hydrated for his game. This is very important if you are driving four or five hours to a tournament weekend and your player must hit the ice right after checking into the hotel.

You know this scenario: The alarm goes off at 4:30 a.m.; thank goodness you packed the car the night before. You grab your coffee and breakfast, maybe a banana and a hard-boiled egg (my favorite to keep me awake and alert on the road). Next, you wake your still-sleepy hockey player. He awakes with more energy than you have because, if your player is like mine, 4:30 a.m. on a travel hockey weekend is AWESOME! Your player is so pumped for the games that he doesn't want to eat. That is why you must pack a food bin for the car. If you are like me, the first-aid kit was packed right alongside the hockey bags, sticks, and jerseys the night before. Now it is time to focus on the food bin.

For the seasoned hockey mom this is easy—second nature. For the new hockey mom, it is easy. Stock a cooler with fruit, water, juices, and protein foods that your player likes. Here is an example of what I pack in my cooler for a road trip:

- Water bottles

- Juice bottles
- Chocolate milk (in the small boxes that you don't have to refrigerate)
- Apples
- Grapes (make small individual containers)
- Bananas
- Cheese sticks
- Beef jerky
- Goldfish (My younger son loves these.)
- A jar of peanut butter (or any nut butter)
- Crackers (My older son likes graham crackers with peanut butter.)
- Granola bars
- Yogurt tubes (Greek or regular)
- Homemade mini banana muffins
- Homemade oatmeal cookies
- Sandwiches on whole-wheat bread with ham, cheese, lettuce, and a small amount of mayonnaise or other dressing

I do not pack all of this food every time, but this gives you an idea of the foods I have on hand, or make, to pack for our trip weekends.

Remember: Food is fuel, and it is as important as the best stick your player uses on the ice.

Give as much time to preparing your hockey food bin as you give to double-checking his bags and the first-aid kit.

When you stop for a meal—and you know you will—whether it is just with your family or with the team, you can help your child make hockey-strong choices at the restaurant. A quick tip: If you are traveling by bus and you know you will be stopping at a restaurant, have one of the parents or team managers call ahead to see if the restaurant can accommodate your team, and even let them know your orders ahead of time if possible. This does take planning, but today, with all the technology we travel with, it is easy to pick a restaurant, look at the menu, and call in an order.

What should you order when you call? In the next section I will go over fueling before a game in detail; for now know that I am focusing on moderate-fat to lower-fat choices. Why? Because four or five hours before game time, you do not want to eat greasy, heavy foods.

I have kept these choices low in fat. You will learn in Step 6: Fueling for Game Day, that high-fat foods will not help your child skate like a champion.

Here are some tips:

- Breakfast is the time to start fueling the body with good high-carbohydrate, lower-fat foods. Breakfast ideas at the hotel, at fast-food restaurants, or at dine-in restaurants:

    - Oatmeal

    - Fruit cups

    - Yogurt

    - Breakfast burrito (one not loaded with sausage and cheese)

    - Pancakes (easy on the syrup; my son likes them with only butter). Syrup will add to the quick energy spike of the pancake, whereas butter will help to slow it down. See the "Carbohydrates" section for information about Glycemic Index versus Glycemic Load Index.

- Fruit smoothies
- Hash browns (Do not choose other fatty foods with hash brown, such as egg, bacon, sausage, etc.)
- Eggs and whole-wheat toast, English muffins, bagels
- Waffles (a favorite of many hockey players)

- Lunches:
  - Sandwiches with lean meats (turkey, chicken, ham)
  - Spaghetti with red sauce
  - Grilled chicken with a baked potato and side salad
  - Steamed vegetables
  - Baked or broiled fish
  - Hamburger (no mayo)
  - Chef salad (go easy on the dressing)
  - Caesar salad
  - Soup and a sandwich
  - Vegetable pizza

- Soft chicken taco (I would not recommend bean tacos on game days; the fiber may lead to intestinal cramps during the game.)
            - Chicken enchilada or fajitas (omit the sour cream and cheese)
    - Dinner:
        - Baked fish, chicken, or turkey with rice, potato, and a steamed vegetable
        - Stir-fry chicken and vegetables with rice
        - Lean red meat with a baked potato and vegetables
        - Spaghetti and red sauce
        - Soup in a bread bowl
        - Many noodle and rice dishes (opt for red sauces over cream sauces)

Eating out is a necessity when traveling. With a little planning, you will always make great hockey-strong choices for your player, and he will learn this important skill, which will stay with him when he leaves home for high school or college hockey.

If travel eating has been a challenge for you in the past, I hope you have learned that eating out doesn't have to mean high-fat, high-sugar choices. You can make great food choices when you are on the go. Whether it is your first tournament weekend or the championship tournament weekend, eat like a champion!

Step 6

Fueling for Game Day

Back in the "Carbohydrates" section I started to teach you about carbohydrates and how many grams were in different types of food. It is important to know which foods are good sources of carbohydrates to eat before competition. I know you have told your children, "Don't eat that sugar; it will make you hyper," and of course they want to eat it. There is some truth to this statement. Sugar is quick energy, and you learned in the "Carbohydrates" section that 30 minutes to an hour before game time your child needs 15–30 grams of carbohydrates. But not pure sugar carbohydrates, like Pixy Stix and Tootsie Rolls. These candies may give your child the proper amount of carbohydrates, but his energy will not last. I remember when our Squirt team was playing in a tournament and the sponsoring team graciously greeted our team with a big bowl of candy and bottles of Gatorade.

A very nice gesture, until I glanced into the bowl: Pixy Stix, Tootsie Rolls, and SweeTARTS. Oh no!!! I went straight to the coach and said, "Please tell me you are not going to allow the players to eat that candy before the game," and the coach yelled, "No candy before the game!" Thank goodness; all I could see in my head was a bunch of rapid-skating hockey players for the first 10 minutes, and then I imagined a bunch of skaters that needed a nap. Carbohydrates are a great source of energy, but you must know how to choose the foods that provide quick energy and lasting energy.

Now is the time to put to use the information you learned in Step 2 about the carbohydrates. Remember: Foods with a high Glycemic Index number give you energy quickly but can cause you to lose steam fast. That bowl of candy would have been a disaster, but a banana, grapes, or cinnamon raisin toast will provide quick energy and lasting energy.

Let's get specific and look at how to fuel before practice.

4–6 Hours Before Practice

Now is the time to "top off the tank" with great food. More than likely this will be your child's school lunch. It is important for him to have meal rich in carbohydrates, moderate protein, and moderate fat. An example of a power lunch would be a sandwich on whole-wheat bread: turkey, chicken, lean ham, or lean beef with a slice of cheese, lettuce, tomato, and mustard. Add a fruit, milk, and a cookie or baked chips. It is important to watch the fat because the body can't readily use fat for energy.

2 Hours Before Practice

Fluids. Drink 2 cups (500 ml) of water. Your skater doesn't have to drink the water all at once; sipping on a bottle filled with water is fine.

30–60 Minutes Before Practice

50 grams of carbohydrates and 5–10 grams of protein. Examples: cheese stick and grapes, nut butter on a bagel, or yogurt and fruit.

10–20 Minutes Before Practice

1 cup of water

During Practice

Take sips of water throughout practice.

30–45 Minutes After Practice

It is important to refuel with 1 gram of carbohydrate per kilogram of weight and 0.2–0.5 grams of protein per kilogram of weight. Here is an example: A 10-year-old boy weighs 64 pounds (29 kg). He needs 29 grams carbohydrates and 6–14 grams of protein. If he likes chocolate milk this is a great refueling drink.

Here are some general guidelines regarding foods to *avoid* before, during, and after practices and games.

Pre-Exercise

- High-fat foods (high-fat meats, heavy sauces/creams, fried foods, buttery foods, desserts)

- High-fiber foods (cruciferous vegetables: broccoli, cauliflower, cabbage; high-fiber whole grains (any bread or cereal containing 3g of fiber or more is considered a good source of fiber, and this may cause gastric distress while running or skating)); buttery foods; desserts; large quantities of nut butters, nuts, and seeds

- Carbonated beverages and sugary beverages

During Exercise

- High-fat foods (high-fat meats, heavy sauces/creams, fried foods, buttery foods, desserts)

- High-fiber foods (cruciferous vegetables: broccoli, cauliflower, cabbage; high-fiber whole grains (any bread or cereal containing 3grams of fiber or more is considered a good source of fiber, and this may cause gastric distress while running or skating)); buttery foods; desserts; large quantities of nut butters, nuts, and seeds

- High-protein foods (meats, dairy, high-protein energy bars)

- Fluids containing more than 8 percent carbohydrate (juice, soda, sweet tea, energy drinks, etc.)

Post Exercise
- High-fat foods (high-fat meats, heavy sauces/creams, fried foods, buttery foods, desserts)
- High-fiber foods (cruciferous vegetables: broccoli, cauliflower, cabbage; high-fiber whole grains (any bread or cereal containing 3g of fiber or more is considered a good source of fiber, and this may cause gastric distress while running or skating)), buttery foods; desserts; large quantities of nut butters, nuts, and seeds
- Fluids containing more than 8 percent carbohydrate (juice, soda, sweet tea, energy drinks, etc.)

Step 7
Time to Organize

Kitchen Tour

I am going to help you stock your kitchen with great choices for your skater. This is the best way to make sure you have hockey-supportive foods available all the time. Ready? Go ahead and open your pantry. Have no fear—I can't see what you have in there.

Let's begin with the cereals. In the "Carbohydrates" section you learned carbohydrates are the body's go-to source for fuel. Cereals are great to have on hand to mix and match for a dry ,crunchy snack or for a quick breakfast. The best choices for you are the ones that contain less than 10 grams of sugar per serving. Take a moment and read the labels. Go ahead, take out each box one at a time, and see what you have on hand. Don't panic if you do not have any foods that have 10 grams or less.

This can be a new goal for you, and you can enlist the help of your children. You can play a game in the grocery store: How many cereals can you find that have 10 grams of sugar or less? My sons like learning about healthy choices, even at 10 and 12.

Do you have an overabundance of chips, packaged cookies, and cake-type treats? These foods are okay. After all, most children enjoy these types of treats. I encourage you to make these occasional foods. Why? Because when children (and adults, for that matter) see chips, cookies, and baked foods around, those are the foods they choose for snacks. You may want to try keeping these foods in tins that you can't see through. This will allow you to keep the treats on hand, and maybe your child will not reach for them as soon as he opens the pantry door.

Remember this is the time to build a great foundation for your child, and learning to choose healthy foods is a brick in that foundation. So what do you choose in place?? My family loves homemade popcorn—not microwave, but the old-fashioned popcorn kernels in the pan with oil. This makes a fresh, crunchy, snack that's very low in additives. You can use any flavors you choose: salt, pepper, Parmesan cheese, garlic and onion powders, and different herbs. Be creative! Allow the popcorn to cool, and then place it in individual Ziploc bags. Now you have grab-and-go snacks for school or when you're running out the door.

Do you have pasta and red sauces on hand? If so, great. Pasta is fantastic meal a few hours before practice. Pasta provides your child with great carbohydrates to fuel his muscles throughout the practice, and it is a good source of iron. When choosing your red sauces, read the labels. Sugar may be a common ingredient because the addition of sugar helps to cut down on the acidity of the tomato sauce, but you don't need high-fructose corn syrup and sugar. I try to buy the red pasta sauces that contain the fewest ingredients. Remember: If your grandmother wouldn't recognize some of the ingredients in the pasta sauce, it would be a good idea to keep looking, or you could make your own pasta sauce. (It is easier than you think.)

Let's move to your refrigerator. Take a breath and open it up. What do you see? Remember that I can't see what you see. If you were to open up my refrigerator, the giant water dispenser on the left might catch your attention first. I encourage you to keep water readily available and easy for your child to serve himself. In addition, you can create a shelf of fruits and vegetables that are ready to eat. You may be thinking, *Where do I find the time to cut up fruits and vegetables?* Fear not: You can buy prepackaged fruits and vegetables in the produce section of most grocery stores. I have learned and observed my sons for many years. If I have bags of chips available, they will choose the chips for snacks, especially my 10-year-old. However, if I have fruit available they will eat the fruit, or chow down on salad. Believe it or not, if I have salad bags in the refrigerator, they will eat them. No lie!

How is your freezer stocked? Ready-to-use frozen vegetables are great! I love those large bags of vegetables that come with a seasoning package, and so do my sons. Just add stir-fried chicken and rice, and you have dinner in about 30 minutes. If you are like many hockey moms, you love your slow cooker. Take time on your non-travel weekends to prepare a few slow cooker freezer meals. Just place your choice of meat, potatoes, onions, garlic, and carrots (or your vegetable of choice) in a freezer bag and freeze. Voila! You have a meal ready to place in your slow cooker. Just add about ½ cup of liquid (water or broth) and seasonings, and you will come home to a warm dinner on those hectic days.

Okay, what else is in there? If you are like me you are bound to have some kind of ice cream (regular, not low fat). And my sons love popsicles. I have several popsicle sets. We make our own when we want them, and we choose the juices. This is a great way to have popsicles and cut down on the added sugar. We love Juicy Juice popsicles. Don't forget to have ice cubes on hand for smoothies. When fruits are on sale ("buy one, get one free" strawberries and blueberries, for example), stock up. Wash the strawberries, cut them in half, and place them in a single layer on a cookie sheet lined with wax paper. Place the cookie sheet in the freezer and allow the strawberries to freeze solid, then you can place them in Ziploc bags for icy-cold smoothies when you want them. You can do the same with blueberries. I peel and slice bananas into rounds and freeze them the same way. Try a frozen banana and strawberry smoothie with water for the base liquid. The frozen fruit gives an ice cream consistency.

I haven't mentioned breads. My family keeps our breads on top of the refrigerator in a bread bin. I tend to buy whole-wheat or honey-wheat bread for the family. To ensure you are truly buying whole-wheat bread, read the label. The first ingredient should be whole-wheat flour. Ingredients on all food labels are listed in order of amount used. If you see whole-wheat flour, water, sugar, wheat gluten, etc., you know the first three ingredients are the most prevalent. Sugar is needed in many breads to feed the yeast so the dough will rise. I do not choose bread that contains sugar and high-fructose corn syrup. You can see that picking out cereals and breads can be a similar process.

Follow the same guidelines when picking out your crackers and premade cookies. The shorter the ingredients list, the better.

***

I hope that wasn't too scary. If you found foods you don't want, go ahead and use them up. It takes time to learn and practice new buying habits. Involve your family and teach them at the same time. You may find it is easier than you think.

To help you stay focused at the grocery store I have included a shopping list:

Carbohydrates: Hockey Fuel (Starches, Dairy, and Fruit)

Starches

- Breads (whole-wheat)
- Baking potatoes
- Sweet potatoes
- Boiling potatoes
- Pasta (whole-wheat)
- Rice (brown, white, or wild)
- Legumes (black beans, navy beans, kidney beans, lentils)
- Corn
- Peas

Fruits

- Fresh fruit (all varieties)
- Fruit juice with no high-fructose corn syrup
- Fruit cups (packed in juice, not syrup)

Cereals

- Total
- Wheaties
- Special K
- Multigrain Cheerios
- Cheerios
- Kashi Go Lean
- Kashi Indigo Morning
- Shredded Wheat

Dairy

- Milk or milk substitute
- Yogurt (tubes and easy-to-pack containers)
- Kefir

Protein-Rich Foods

Beef	Shrimp	Edamame	Veggie burgers
Chicken	Lobster	Eggs or egg substitute	Venison burgers, jerky, roasts
Pork	Crab		
Salmon	Tuna	Cottage cheese	
Tilapia	Trout	Quinoa	

Healthy Fats

Oils (olive, canola, peanut)

Avocados

Nuts and seeds (peanuts, almonds, pecans, sunflower seeds)

Vegetables

Broccoli	Greens (collard greens, mustard, kale, spinach)	Red bell peppers
Brussels sprouts		Tomatoes
Cabbage	Cucumbers	Squash
Carrots	Green beans	Zucchini
Cauliflower	Mushrooms	
Celery	Parsnips	

Snack Foods

Whole-grain crackers

Baked chips or tortillas

Air-popped popcorn

Recipes

My boys love all of these recipes. You can substitute different types of bread, milk, and meats and meat substitutes (like Veggie Crumblers by Morningstar) for any of the recipes.

Breakfast

I love these breakfast recipes because I can measure out the ingredients the night before and make them in the morning. The Homemade French Toast is very fast, less than five minutes. The waffle batter will keep for two days in the refrigerator. Many times I make the entire waffle recipe and store at least half of it in the refrigerator for breakfast the following day or for afternoon snacks. The waffles make a great after-hockey snack. Serve them with a glass of milk.

Breakfasts can be challenging. Here are two of my favorite recipes:

Homemade French Toast

If you are making this recipe on the morning of a practice, I recommend bread with less than 3 grams of fiber. Remember that fiber can cause cramping during a game or practice. Serve with syrup, or sprinkle with powdered sugar, and add fruit on the side.

Ingredients

- 1 egg
- 1 T. milk
- ½ tsp. vanilla
- 1 dash cinnamon
- 3 slices whole-wheat bread or rye bread

Directions

1. In a medium bowl blend milk and egg.
2. Add vanilla and cinnamon.
3. Dunk bread in milk and egg mixture, one piece at a time.
4. Cook over medium heat in a non-stick skillet sprayed with non-stick spray, or in a skillet with a small amount of oil.

Wake-Up Waffles

Leftover waffles can be stored in a Ziploc bag in the refrigerator for up to two days. Reheat in the microwave or toast in the toaster.

Ingredients

1¾ c. all-purpose flour

1 T. baking powder

¼ tsp. salt

½ c. oil

1¾ c. milk

2 eggs, separated

½ tsp. vanilla

scant ¼ tsp. cinnamon

Directions

1. Preheat waffle iron.
2. Measure and sift together flour, baking powder, and salt, and set aside.
3. Measure oil, milk, and egg yolks into a different bowl, and mix well.
4. Whip egg whites to soft peaks in another bowl.
5. Combine the oil, milk, and egg yolk mix with the flour, baking powder, and salt mixture, and blend well.
6. Mix in vanilla and cinnamon.
7. Fold in whipped egg whites.
8. Cook waffles using about ½ cup of batter per waffle.

Lunch

Stuck for what to pack for lunch? These recipes travel great in a thermos.

Chili Stuffed Potatoes

Add some grated cheese and chopped onions, and enjoy.

Ingredients

- 2 lb. ground beef
- 2 cloves garlic, chopped
- 1 8-oz. can tomato sauce
- 2 T. chili powder
- 1 tsp. ground cumin
- 1 tsp. ground oregano
- 1/2 tsp. salt
- 1/4 tsp. cayenne pepper
- 1 15-oz. can kidney beans, drained and rinsed
- 1 15-oz. can pinto beans, drained and rinsed
- 1 medium-sized baked potato per person

Directions

1. Place the ground beef in a large pot, cook until brown, and drain off excess fat.
2. Add chopped garlic.
3. Add beans, tomato sauce, chili powder, cumin, oregano, salt, and cayenne. Stir together well, cover, and then reduce the heat to low.
4. Simmer for one hour, stirring occasionally. (If the mixture becomes overly dry, add 1/2 cup water at a time as needed.)
5. Split open the baked potato and scoop chili on top of the potato.

Cream Cheese and Spinach Stuffed Chicken

Remember to check the temperature of the chicken before eating. I cook my chicken to 170 degrees F just to be safe. Add a piece of bacon wrapped around each chicken breast if you like, secured with toothpicks.

Add some rice, a side salad, and a beverage, and you have a complete meal.

If you pack this in a thermos, chop up the chicken and send the sauce in a separate container. There are many types of containers that are stored in the freezer before use in a lunch box. I use one of those for the sauce.

Ingredients

3 lb. boneless, skinless chicken breasts

8 oz. regular or low-fat cream cheese

2 c. fresh spinach, finely chopped

2 cloves garlic, chopped

Directions

1. Place individual chicken breasts on a large piece of saran wrap. Fold wrap over chicken and pound with a meat mallet to flatten and enlarge chicken breast. Repeat process for each chicken breast.
2. Place cream cheese in medium size bowl and soften with fork.
3. Mix chopped spinach and garlic into cream cheese.
4. Carefully stuff each chicken breast with cream cheese and spinach mixture, roll up chicken, and secure with toothpicks.
5. Bake in a baking dish for 20 minutes.
6. Once the chicken is cooked, slice into rounds and serve with a dipping sauce of your choosing.

Dinners

Italian Vegetable Soup

I use four garlic cloves when I make this soup.
Serve with crackers, garlic bread, or both! Sprinkle with Parmesan cheese.

Ingredients

1 lb. ground beef	5–6 c. broth
1 c. chopped onion	1 T. parsley
1 c. chopped celery	1 tsp. salt
1 c. chopped carrots	1/2 tsp. oregano
1–4 garlic cloves	1/2 tsp. basil
1 16-oz. can tomatoes, diced	1/4 tsp. pepper
1 16-oz. can beans (red or pinto), not drained	2 c. shredded cabbage
	1 c. cut green beans
1 16-oz. can tomato sauce	1/2 c. pasta
2 c. water	

Directions

1. Brown ground beef in the same pot you will cook your soup in, draining fat while cooking.
2. Sauté onion, celery, carrots, and garlic in a skillet over medium heat 3–5 minutes, stirring frequently.
3. Add sautéed vegetables to ground beef.
4. Add remaining ingredients except pasta, and bring to a boil.

5. Reduce heat and simmer for 30 minutes.
6. Cook pasta in water, and then add cooked pasta to beef and vegetable mixture.

Tips from Kim:

I don't use bouillon cubes. I buy broth in the carton and use one carton per recipe. If you want to reduce the sodium in your soup, buy reduced-sodium or sodium-free broth. I use chicken broth. Draining and rinsing the canned beans before adding them to the soup will reduce the sodium. Be sure to replace the liquid you drained off the beans with 1 cup of water. You can also substitute any other meat or veggie crumbles by Morningstar for the ground beef. In a pinch, if you don't have canned tomatoes, canned pasta sauce works well. You will not find 16-ounce cans in the grocery stores, so buy 14 1/2-ounce cans. I choose to leave all the sodium in this recipe because my sons enjoy this soup after hockey.

Baked Chicken on Top of Potatoes

This recipe is simple to prepare and yummy. You will not need to add any butter to the potatoes. Base the number of pieces of chicken you use on the number of people you are feeding, and how many pieces of chicken each person will eat.

Ingredients

5 baking potatoes

1 T. olive oil

4 leg and thigh combination chicken pieces

paprika to taste

salt to taste

2 lbs. frozen green beans

Directions

1. Wash and quarter potatoes.
2. Place olive oil in a large bowl, add potatoes, and mix.
3. Place oil-coated potatoes in an 11 x 13 inch baking dish.
4. Place chicken pieces in the bowl containing the oil; add more oil if needed. Turn chicken to coat.
5. Place chicken on top of potatoes in the baking dish. Sprinkle with paprika and salt if desired.
6. Bake at 400 degrees F for 40 minutes or until the chicken reaches 170 degrees F internal temperature.
7. Cook green beans in water.

Vegetarian Recipes

Quinoa Risotto with Spinach and Parmesan Cheese

Ingredients

1 T. olive oil

½ yellow onion, diced small

1 garlic clove, minced fine

1 c. quinoa, rinsed well

18 oz. vegetable stock

1–2 c. fresh spinach, chopped

½ carrot, peeled and shredded

½ c. mushrooms, sliced

¼ c. grated Parmesan cheese

½ tsp. salt

¼ tsp. pepper, ground

Directions

1. In a saucepan, heat olive oil over medium heat. Add onion and sauté until translucent, about 4 minutes.
2. Add garlic and quinoa, and cook for about 1 minute, stirring occasionally. Do not let garlic brown.
3. Add stock and bring to a boil. Reduce heat to low, and simmer until quinoa is almost tender to the bite but not hard in the center, about 12 minutes. (The mixture will be somewhat liquid.)
4. Stir in spinach, carrot, and mushrooms, and simmer until the quinoa grains have turned from white to translucent.
5. Stir in cheese, and season with salt and pepper. Serve immediately.

Sesame-Crusted Tofu

Ingredients

1 lb. firm tofu, drained	3 T. bread crumbs
¼ c. milk	2 T. sesame seeds
2 eggs, lightly beaten	1 T. black sesame seeds
½ tsp. salt	½ tsp. sesame or olive oil
¼ tsp. pepper	4 scallions for garnish

Directions

1. Cut tofu into 12 slices. In a dry non-stick pan, sauté tofu on medium-low heat about 5 minutes on each side. (The tofu will be lightly browned on each side and lose some of its liquid.)
2. In a bowl, whisk together milk, eggs, ¼ tsp. of the salt, and pepper until well blended. On a large plate, combine and mix well the bread crumbs, sesame seeds, black sesame seeds, and remaining salt.
3. Dip tofu slices into milk mixture, then dredge in the bread crumb and sesame seed mixture.
4. In a non-stick pan, heat oil on medium heat. Sauté tofu slices, turning once, until lightly browned, about 3 minutes on each side. Time will vary depending on whether you are using a gas or electric stove. Add scallions, and sauté.
5. Garnish tofu with the scallions, and serve hot.

Tabboulleh

Tabboulleh makes a great side dish or protein-rich snack.

Ingredients

- 1 c. vegetable stock
- 1 c. bulgur wheat, fine-grind
- 2 c. chopped tomatoes
- ½ of 6- to 8-inch cucumber, peeled, seeded, and diced small
- ¼ c. lemon juice, fresh
- ¼ c. parsley, fresh, finely chopped
- 3 T. mint, finely chopped
- 2 T. extra-virgin olive oil
- 2 scallions, finely chopped
- 1 T. lemon zest
- 1 clove garlic, minced
- ¾ tsp. salt
- ¼ tsp. pepper, freshly ground

Directions

1. Place bulgur wheat in a large stainless steel bowl.
2. In a small saucepan, bring vegetable stock to a boil. Pour boiling stock over bulgur wheat and let stand until bulgur wheat is tender and *all* liquid has been absorbed. Chill in refrigerator.
3. When bulgur wheat is chilled, add all remaining ingredients and serve.

Power Snacks

Banana and Peanut Butter Smoothie

This is the smoothie my son drinks one hour before he goes to his weight-training sessions.

Ingredients

1 banana, ripe, cut up

1 c. milk

1/3 c. vanilla ice cream

2 T. peanut butter

Directions

1. Place all ingredients in a blender and blend.

Celery Stuffed with Peanut Butter or Almond Butter

Wash celery. Cut large ribs into 3 or 4 pieces and fill with the nut butter of your choice.

Protein Wrap-Ups

This is super simple. Take any type of cheese stick your skater likes; wrap it with a piece of ham, turkey, or chicken; and enjoy. Add some fruit and water or milk, and you have a great pre-practice snack.

For vegetarian skaters: Snack on nut butter on graham crackers with fruit and water or milk (milk substitute).

Sample Meal Plan 2,400 Calories for 8- to 12-Year-Olds

This is only a sample. Youth ice hockey players may need more or less, depending on their body size, age, and practice schedule.

Daily serving amounts from the food groups include: 8 grains, 3 c. veggies, 2 c. fruit, 3 c. dairy, 6.5–7 oz. protein

- **Breakfast:** 1 frozen waffle or 4-inch homemade waffle, sprinkled with powdered sugar or served with 1 T. syrup (measured in a 1-ounce medicine cup so your child will not soak the waffle), piece of fruit, and 1 cup milk

- **Morning snack:** 1 granola bar and water

- **Lunch:** Sandwich on 2 slices whole-wheat bread, 2–3 oz. lean beef, ham, or turkey with mustard, pretzels, cookie, fruit, and water or milk

- **After-school snack** (this can work as a before-practice snack, too, if practice is about two or three hours after school): 1 cup cooked pasta noodles with red sauce, 1 cup cooked vegetables (green beans, carrots, peas) or a tossed salad, and milk

- **Dinner:** 3–4 oz. meat or fish (equivalent to the size of a deck of cards), grilled, broiled, baked, or poached, ½ cup cooked starchy vegetable (corn, peas, lima beans, etc.), 1 piece of bread, a tossed salad, and water or milk

- **Dessert:** ½ cup ice cream, or 1 small slice of cake or pie, or 2 cookies with milk

You will notice I have listed milk more than three times. Aim for at least three servings of milk or yogurt throughout the day. My sons prefer water with their lunch and drink milk at home.

If your child is vegetarian remember to include legumes (pinto, black, navy, and garbanzo beans) for protein. Quinoa is an excellent source of complete protein, too. You can usually find it in the pasta aisle of the grocery store.

Conclusion

You have come to the end of the book. I hope you have learned a lot. All of this information aside, this is what you have to know: It is crucial to keep your youth hockey player well hydrated and fed. I hope by now you know it's not enough just to eat and drink; it matters *what* you eat and drink. The food your child eats influences his performance on the ice and in the classroom. It is one thing to learn and understand this information; it is a completely different task to apply this information. Problems always come up. One of my favorites is when you stop at a restaurant on your way to a game. There are times when a parent will look at a menu and say, "How do I know what to feed my skater?" I can tell you that more than once I have been asked that very question by some of the hockey moms on our team.

This is my passion and specialty. I can create an individualized plan for your youth hockey star. E-mail me at Kim@HockeyMomRD.com to get started.

Resources

"Carbonated Beverages, Dietary Calcium, the Dietary Calcium/Phosphorus Ratio, and Bone Fractures in Girls and Boys," *Journal of Adolescent Health*, Volume 15, 1994.

NUTR, by McGuire/Beerman, 2013.

Sports Nutrition Guidebook, 5th edition, by Nancy Clark.

Vitamins and Minerals Demystified, by Steve Blake, 2007.

Websites

www.huffingtonpost.com/2012/04/27/vitamin-c-foods_n_1457397.html

http://calorielab.com/index.html

Unleash the Champion in Your Youth Hockey Star!

Discover the secrets to help your child be a champion on the ice and in the classroom. During your phone "chalk talk" sessions you will find out how to apply action steps to unleash the future NHL player in your youth hockey star.

Do you want your child to…

- Avoid a midmorning energy crash in school?
- Have a body well fueled to hit the ice?
- Have lasting energy on the ice?
- Build stronger skating muscle?
- Learn how food can be as important as sharp skates and his hockey stick?

If you answered YES, get started at HockeyMomRD.com and grab your three power recipes. There you will also find other tips and resources to make your hockey player a star.

Testimonials

"Recommended Her to My Hockey Family!"

I received a specialized plan from Kim for my first-year Bantam just before the season began. She included allergies/preferences as well as late adjustments for dislike of all things peanut. It has truly helped us all make positive changes toward better meal plans that incorporate the specialized needs of a hockey player. I couldn't be more pleased with the plan and the personalized service I received, and I have recommended her to all my hockey family! Thanks to Hockey Mom RD!

~ Shelleigh Killian

"As a Physician, I Am Impressed!"

My daughter lives by the plan Kim worked out for her this fall and I can't say thank you enough! Maggie is away from home at the Ontario Hockey Academy and has a rigorous strength training routine and on-ice practice every single day. Kim gave her great practical guidelines on how to choose foods to meet her nutritional needs and food preferences specific to her situation. As a mother I am so glad she has Kim's guidance away from me. As a physician I am impressed by Kim's total approach and in-depth plans. I commend Hockey Mom RD and recommend her evaluation and advice for youth athletes in any sport.

~ Elizabeth Blair, MD, PhD

"Kim Created Thoughtful and Detailed Plans"

Our boys have been playing (and loving!) hockey since long before they could spell their own names. Once we became a hockey family, there was no looking back! One piece of the puzzle that has always been difficult for us as parents is nutrition. Are our boys eating enough of the right foods? How long before a game should they have a snack and what should that snack be? Kim created thoughtful and detailed plans for both of my boys that answered every question we ever had and so many more. We feel so much more confident as hockey parents that our boys are fueled up and hydrated so that they can play to their full potential and have as much fun as possible on and off the ice! Did I mention that Kim is registered dietician, a college professor working with student athletes, as well as a hockey mom and player? Well, really, what more could you ask for?

~ Ellie Petrov, hockey mom and blogger (www.Creative-Geekery.com)

Made in the USA
Coppell, TX
15 September 2023